Kita Mean is the queen of camp and winner of *RuPaul's Drag Race Down Under* Season One. An owner of two drag venues, Kita is a boss bitch entrepreneur who has graced stages all around the world. With over a decade of experience tucked away, Kita Mean is guaranteed to leave you grinning!

Life in Lashes

KITA MEAN

Life in Lashes

HarperCollins*Publishers*

HarperCollins*Publishers*
Australia • Brazil • Canada • France • Germany • Holland • India
Italy • Japan • Mexico • New Zealand • Poland • Spain • Sweden
Switzerland • United Kingdom • United States of America

First published in 2022
by HarperCollins*Publishers* (New Zealand) Limited
Unit D1, 63 Apollo Drive, Rosedale, Auckland 0632, New Zealand
harpercollins.co.nz

Written with Eli Matthewson

Copyright © Outrageous Entertainment Limited 2022

A catalogue record for this book is available from the National Library of
New Zealand

ISBN 978 1 7755 4222 3 (pbk)
ISBN 978 1 7754 9236 8 (ebook)
ISBN 978 1 4607 4555 7 (international audiobook)

Cover design by Hazel Lam, HarperCollins Design Studio
Cover photography and author photograph by Garth Badger, Thievery Studio
Typeset in Adobe Garamond Pro by Kirby Jones

Printed and bound by CPI Group (UK) Ltd, Croydon, CR0 4YY

To my mother and father, my brothers and sisters,
my drag mother and my entire drag family. I am eternally
grateful for the love and guidance you've given me.
You believed in me even when I sometimes didn't believe
in myself, so now I am dedicated to working hard and
making you proud. I love you. Let's do this!

CONTENTS

CHAPTER 1

A homecoming queen

I'M GOING TO LET you in on a little secret. For every season of *Drag Race*, they film multiple endings, in order to keep the actual results of the show hidden from everyone, including the competitors, until the finale airs on TV. It's a way of ensuring the show isn't spoiled by leaks, and each season only a select few people know the real outcome before the show airs.

On the day we filmed the finale in Auckland, we all got to wear the crown and parade around with the sceptre, living out our total fantasy, but we wouldn't find out who the crown and sceptre would belong to until four months later when the show finally aired.

In a perfect, virus-free world, on the night of the finale of *RuPaul's Drag Race Down Under*, I would have been in Sydney with my *Down Under* sisters. Karen, Art, Scarlet and I would have ended our intense, bumpy but seriously rewarding journey together as we found out who of the four of us was the first crowned *Down Under* queen.

The world, however, is not perfect or virus free. Having poured every resource I had and every ounce of energy and passion I could muster into my run on the show, it became clear I would not be joining my fellow top-four queens for the finale. We would not be together when we found out who would be crowned because an evil queen known as Delta Variant had arrived and she seemed desperate to stomp her stilettos all over my dreams.

When it came time for the finale to air, I had absolutely no confidence that I would be the winner of *Drag Race*. I figured I'd had an okay run – I'd made myself proud at times and disappointed myself at others. While I knew I had crushed the final lip-sync and the last challenge, I still couldn't believe that I would overcome the Australian queens, whose huge profiles made me feel like a Make-a-Wish kid who had been gifted the opportunity to hang with the big dogs.

Even as I watched the show, I saw myself as more of a background character, chiming away in the back of the shots, getting my work done and not drawing a hell of a lot of attention to myself. With a bit of luck, I thought, maybe I'd be invited back for some kind of All Stars show where I'd be able to push myself to stand out more, to make sure people would notice me.

In the week leading up to the finale though, it became very clear that people *had* noticed me, and they really loved what I did. The likes and retweets on the #TeamKitaMean pictures on social media were going ballistic. People were writing about how much they loved my classic, campy approach to drag, about how the show had never seen a winner like me, a true fashion-clown, someone who truly embodied the word 'camp' and competed with a relentlessly positive spirit. It was only then that I allowed myself to wonder whether that moment I'd got to prance around with the crown and sceptre might just have been for real …

Still, no matter how overwhelming the social media response was, I struggled to see myself emerging as the winner. The other queens were such powerhouses. Art already had a show made by the network who made *Drag Race*, Karen was a name drag fans around the world had known for years, and Scarlet had a staggering three challenge wins against my single one.

Maybe it's the small-poppy New Zealander in me, but I told myself not to get too big for my boots. Just like when I get served food on an aeroplane, I kept my expectations low so I wouldn't be disappointed. Still, whoever was crowned, I wanted to be with my sisters to celebrate. I wanted to finish this surrounded by the new family I had gained through the show.

Our corner of the world had enjoyed a Covid-free few months, so a handy travel bubble had opened up allowing Kiwis and Aussies to travel freely between the two countries.

Then, just 24 hours before I was due to leave for Sydney, our luck ran out. Covid was back in Australia and the travel bubble had burst just in time to ruin the end of my *Drag Race* journey. Bugger it!

Suddenly, I had no plans for watching the end of the show. There was no official event or party to go to, and it was looking like I would just be on my couch, in my track pants, watching the big finale all by myself – unless I could bring the party to me …

* * *

'All right everyone. Hand me your phones right now. They are going into this bucket, and you'll get them back at the end of the episode. Now, bitches!'

That was Amanda Pain, absolutely in her element bossing us all around. Amanda was a producer on *Drag Race Down Under* and the earlier (and much more low-budget) Kiwi show *House of Drag*. I had invited all of my favourite people around to my house to watch the finale together, and, even though she wasn't technically on the clock, she had taken it on herself to produce my party.

The finale was due to air at 8.30 pm on Saturday on TVNZ 2, but the network dropped it on their streaming service at 6 pm, which meant anyone watching it would be able to fast forward to the end then name the winner on social media. Amanda wanted me to watch the result live, to see it fresh with no warning, which is why she confiscated all of our phones for the night.

After a week during which my confidence had been going up and down like a roller coaster, I had no idea what to expect. Then I heard RuPaul herself say those magical words, 'The winner of *Drag Race Down Under*, and Down Under's next drag superstar is … Kita Mean!'

My friends had kept telling me that the victory was mine, but I still didn't believe it. Tears streamed down my face like a dam had burst. I couldn't believe that this little boy from Auckland had grown up to achieve his greatest dream.

From a shy little child, ashamed of his weight and terrified of putting himself out there, he had become a queen whose crazy, campy drag had captured the hearts of fans all around the world. If someone had told that little kid from Cockle Bay what was ahead for him, he would never have believed it.

CHAPTER 2

It all comes back to Cockle

YES, YOU READ THAT right: this little fairy was born in a place called Cockle Bay. If my parents wanted a straight son, they definitely picked the wrong place to start my life!

Cockle Bay is in Auckland's eastern suburbs, about half an hour's drive from the city centre, and it's probably better known for producing accountants and plumbers than *Drag Race* superstars. The place is idyllic, but in a bit of a creepy *Pleasantville* way, and there isn't a whole heap to do there. Everything looks almost too perfect to be real. The streets and the playgrounds are almost too clean and the mothers walking their children in prams are gorgeous but with the energy of *The Stepford Wives*.

I was the third of my parents' five children, and my dad had a son, Craig, from a previous marriage. By the time I arrived, my parents thought they knew exactly how to raise a child, but even from when I was tiny, I always found a way to stand out from the rest.

There's one story about me as little baby Nick that is always told when my family gets back together. I will warn you now to put your scepticism aside, because this one gets a little supernatural.

There was always a kind of spiritual presence in the house we lived in on Tainui Road, and we found out years later that it was built near an ancient Māori cemetery. That's not something my parents knew when they bought the place, but it provides a possible explanation for the supernatural events that occurred there.

My parents, who have long since divorced and don't agree on much, are completely united on this: they both saw me glow. Not in the 'Wow, what skincare range do you use?' way, but actually glowing – like a human baby light bulb.

I had only spent a few months on this earth when my mum, Bridget, came upstairs to check on me. She walked into the nursery and saw me lying asleep with what she describes as a glowing ring around my entire body.

Of course, she immediately freaked out and screamed for my father: 'Robert! Something creepy is happening to Nick! Robert! Come up here right now!'

Once in the room, he stared at me, flabbergasted. He could see the glowing ring too.

They didn't know what to do so Mum picked me up and, as soon as she did, the glowing stopped – like the opposite of the Midas touch!

Once I'd gone back to being a normal, glow-less baby, my parents searched the room to see if the window had let light through at an angle that made me look particularly radiant, or if maybe the baby monitor had fallen into my cot and was illuminating me somehow … but there was nothing. They couldn't find a single thing in that room that could have made me look like that, and they maintain to this very day that something weird or magical was happening.

And hey, I'll take it! Who wouldn't want to claim that they were born with a natural glow? It seems that right from the jump I was finding ways to outshine everyone around me!

While I may have started out with a bright glow, the true glow-up from Nick to Kita Mean would take years and plenty of cockle-ups along the way.

* * *

Sometimes my mother likes to make out that she and my father were in some kind of arranged marriage, and while that might be her truth, it is not *the* truth. While she might have been encouraged into the relationship by her family, no one was forced into anything. One of the things she and my father had in common was that both of their families had money.

Mum's family probably fitted more with the typical idea of a rich family. They were what some would describe as hoity-toity, with a real reverence for the achievements of their relations. My mother's grandfather was the Speaker of the House in Parliament, something they all love to bring up whenever possible.

My dad's family weren't from the same kind of high-class lineage. Theirs was 'new money' made by investing in the right business at the right time. They owned the *Evening Standard* in Palmerston North, and the newsprint industry was still positively booming when my parents first got together.

As newsprint was in the family's blood, my dad ran two businesses that occupied a particular subsection of the newspaper industry. First, he ran his own printing business with an old-fashioned, single-colour, manual press, which was used to print newspapers back in the day.

His second business, however, was slightly more niche. Before digital printing and cheap photography became widespread, when a company wanted to advertise their products, they would need images to be hand-drawn by an artist. My dad, who was not an artist himself, would commission the artworks of whatever was being sold, which could be anything from VCR players to canned food. These images would then be used in advertisements in the newspapers he printed.

Now, I'm sure some of you are thinking, 'God, how old is this Kita bitch if her dad was getting cans of Coke painted for the newspaper ads!?' But the truth is I'm not *that* old. My dad just hung on to his business even as new technology meant it was completely outdated.

While their families didn't 'arrange' their marriage, they certainly weren't opposed to the union when my parents met and started dating. Dad maintains that my mother's mum was particularly keen for them to marry, and my mum says she had no choice in the matter. Whatever the case, I can't remember many times when theirs felt like a particularly happy marriage.

They did, however, have things in common. They are both massive people-pleasers. To this day, Mum is always thinking of others. She works in aged-care and has always done jobs that support those who need it. She's incredibly generous in her work, but she also loves to receive acknowledgment for what she does.

She had a tough relationship with her own mother and sister, and it was easy to see why. My grandmother was as posh as they come. Everything she did was proper, which meant everything other people did was not. She was always talking about teaching her grandchildren to become decent humans. 'Bring the children to Raumati Beach and I'll show them how to make an actual apple pie,' she'd say, as if my mother wasn't capable of teaching us anything herself.

Because my mum didn't get the sort of affirmation she craved from her own mother, she needs a little bit more positive reinforcement from other people. When she gives me a present, she'll ask at least 20 times if I like it, as she needs to feel sure that she's done the right thing.

Dad is a different type of people-pleaser. He loves his work, so much so that, as children, we didn't see that much of him. And his refusal to move with the times, paired with his people-pleasing intentions, got him into more trouble.

Dad didn't want to let down any of his employees. He never wanted to give them bad news, so he just wouldn't tell them anything – and things got pretty bad in the newsprinting business. He would take the hits himself while the employees drove around in company cars they didn't need. He didn't want to cut back their salaries, so he cut his own. He treated the impending failure of his business like most governments treat climate change – by denying there was even a problem – but the financial sea levels were rising around him, and fast.

I don't know whether he truly believed that his style of printing would come back into fashion, or whether he was just too stubborn to admit defeat, but the lifestyle we had become accustomed to faded away very quickly. The big, two-storey house on Tainui Road in Cockle Bay had to be sold and we moved into a much smaller, rougher house with a leaking roof in Howick. As this happened, it seemed as though my mother had already checked out of the marriage even though she didn't leave right away.

* * *

My mother, Bridget, liked things to look perfect. When Mum spoke, she didn't sound like a New Zealander; she was all posh vowels and crisp consonants, almost more English than Kiwi, and she was always reminding us to speak in the 'proper' way. We got feedback on the way we talked every single day: 'It's pic-ture not pit-cher. If it's more than one woman, you pronounce it "wimmin".'

We weren't allowed to sit on our beds once we'd made them because we would mess up the sheets. A mug without a coaster underneath it? That was a criminal offence. She was the height of decorum, one baby step away from drinking her tea with her pinky out.

She used to put me and my four siblings in matching outfits, taking her inspiration from the way Princess Diana dressed her two sons. She'd take us all down to Cockle Bay Beach in these outfits to have posh family portraits taken. No matter what was going on inside our house, she made sure we looked like a perfect, harmonious unit.

We weren't always easy to deal with, especially because there was almost ten years difference between the eldest, Matthew, and the youngest, Sophie – with me as the piggy in the middle.

Mum would sometimes get babysitters in to help carry the load. Matthew, Sophie and I were all little gremlins, but

I was the worst of the bunch. I would behave like an absolute brat on purpose so that each new babysitter would quit or, even better, get fired. Whenever I get trolled by awful people online, I always think about how I once behaved the exact same way to our babysitters.

I loved being overly dramatic and would always act out when we were in other people's care. 'You're not my real mum!' was one of my favourite phrases, and every babysitter got to hear me say it at least once. I would be absolutely feeling myself as I yelled it across the room before adding, 'And you never will be!'

To make sure our caregivers got in trouble, we would utilise the perfect weapon. We had this massive, red, portable tape recorder, which was powered by eight of those giant, chunky old batteries that were incredibly fat but still only powered your toys for about an hour.

We used the tape recorder to catch out a particularly annoying (to us, even though she was probably lovely) babysitter named Kirsten. We pressed record, hid it in a duffel bag then tried to trick her into saying something incriminating. After a while of us being absolutely disobedient, she finally dropped an F-bomb. Bam! We'd got her. Da da da-da da, FUCK OFF!

If Kirsten is reading this – I'm sorry. (But it was fun getting to live my *Home Alone* pranking fantasy, so I don't have any regrets really!)

* * *

I have always been a self-identifying fashionista. It was clear from pretty early on that I liked kitting myself out in a great lewk.

There was a dress-up box at my kindergarten that I would pick through, trying on all the best things in there while the other kids played in the sandpit, pretended to be cowboys or threw balls around. Anyone with eyes could see that my interests were slightly different than your average kid, because I never had to fight anyone for the dress-up box. In fact, it was usually just me, by myself, pulling out the outfits and sizing up what I wanted to wear for a few minutes, before I (inevitably) changed into something even more fabulous. After all, every event needs an arrival look, a performance look and an exit look!

We had a dress-up box at home as well, and I raided it almost every day to find the most glamorous thing to put on. My addiction to dressing up became so strong the rest of my family would just refer to it as 'Nick's dress-up box'. To be five years old and already have my name attached to the dress-ups was probably a sign of what was to come!

I was obsessed with the box in a way I never would be about a box again. It didn't interest any of my siblings, which worked fine for me. I would spend hours rotating between bizarre outfits that I, as a five-year-old boy, felt absolutely fierce in. Most of the contents were old clothes and accessories from my mother, and she was a fancy woman so there was some quality stuff in there.

I would occasionally try to speed up the process of her clothes making it into the box. If she had a silk scarf I wanted to try on, I would sneak it out of her drawers and into the box, then just pretend it had always been there. I took from the rich and gave to myself, like a self-serving, very gay Robin Hood.

I'd put on outfits and do little shows for my family. There are photos of me riding around on a Moon Hopper in what I realise now is a deeply problematic headdress, but fortunately I don't think you can cancel toddlers for cultural appropriation. I couldn't possibly have been educated about my outfit choices.

I made my own scarecrow costume and I would stand outside in it, waiting for birds to land on me. I was clearly quite confused about the concept of scarecrows as I thought they were there for birds to come and sit on. My dad took a stealthy Handycam video of me standing, waiting for over 15 minutes while not a single bird took notice of me.

Of course, the dress-up box had a pearl in its collection – one item that stood tall above the rest in its glorious shimmer and gorgeous shape. My sisters had all been flower girls at a wedding, and they had each been made these matching custom dresses in incredibly tacky synthetic gold fabric, with white lace trims and enormous puffy sleeves. They were like 1980s prom dresses but made for children.

What was absolutely iconic about them was that I kept wearing them for years because we had them in three different sizes. As I got older, taller and wider, but not at all wiser, there was still a dress that fitted me. In fact, it was like an upgrade, because, by the time I grew out of them, the one I was ditching had been incredibly well-worn – just by me though. My sisters wore them just the once at the wedding and were done with them, so the newer, bigger dress would be almost untouched. Those dresses were the perfect meeting of camp, kitsch and beauty. They were a true sign of who I was to become and of the aesthetic I would embrace for the rest of my life.

When I went to school, the teacher asked what we wanted to be when we grew up. Most of my class would give the expected answers.

'An astronaut!'

'A cowboy!'

'The president!'

'A firefighter!'

When it came to my turn, I confidently gave a surprising and unique answer: 'A clown!'

That's right, my great dream was to whack on some oversized shoes, paint on a grin and make a fool of myself. Can you imagine what a treat it would be if I got to go back in time and show little Nick what he's up to now? I think he'd love it. I think he'd be pretty stoked that I get to do the silliest job ever in the most fabulous gowns.

Even as a kid, there was a part of me that felt destined for the spotlight. I was always telling Mum and Dad, 'I'm going to be rich and famous one day!' Mum and Dad never actively discouraged these flights of fancy, but I'm sure they thought it was just Nick being Nick.

Maybe because I was his only brother, Matthew was a bit of a bully to me. He would prank me and get me into trouble on purpose. He even used my skills against me.

From an early age, I loved writing lyrics and rhymes. It was a skill that would come in handy in the future, but as a child it got me into trouble. Once, I wrote a nasty rhyme about my mother's friend, who had a big nose, and how her sneezes would blow up houses. Matthew told me to sign my name to it, then he snuck it in the woman's bag when I wasn't looking. It did not go down well.

Matthew also knew exactly how to freak me out. When I was quite young, he told me that I was a werewolf, and that I turned into a wolf when the full moon came around. He told me it had already happened and I'd been turning into a wolf, leaving the house and killing people. I cried and cried, wracked with guilt that I had already committed multiple murders even though I wasn't even eight years old. When the full moon did come, I would force myself to stay awake all night, because I wasn't really keen to kill any more people.

* * *

As my dad's businesses were falling apart, he found a lifeline in one of his side hustles. He'd got to know an old man in England who had written crossword puzzles and supplied them to newspapers all his life. My father made him an offer and managed to acquire every single crossword puzzle that this man had created. Dad then slowly sold those to newspapers around Aotearoa, which made him a small but not insignificant amount of money.

When he met with liquidators as his company was closing down, the liquidator gave my dad a little wink and tried to let him know that if he could move his crossword business into a separate entity, it would not be affected by everything else that was falling down.

My mum was at the meeting and, according to her version of the story, the hints were a little too subtle for Dad. She claims she was the one who picked up on it and managed to save the last little scraps of his business holdings.

'I hear what you're saying, Jonathan, thank you so much,' she told the liquidator, and basically held my dad's hand to get him to sign a form that would keep him and my family afloat.

It's hard to imagine what my dad would have done had he not signed that paper. He sold those crosswords for years, then when they started to feel a bit out of date, he began writing and selling new ones. He was good at it and thrived on designing new and exciting puzzles for readers around the country. He even ended up selling the newspapers sets of horoscopes.

If you've done a crossword or read a horoscope in a New Zealand newspaper at some point during your life, my dad might have designed that crossword or written that horoscope. I just hope you didn't take the horoscope advice too seriously. I can tell you with assurance that the stars weren't telling you anything. Instead, it was Robert Nash from Howick having a go as – I'm sorry to any astrology fans – he completely pulled them out of his ass! Those horoscopes were nothing to do with whether your sun or moon was rising, and everything to do with what mood my dad was in.

Over the years, I've tried to get him to update his skills and learn how to put his crosswords online, but he's remained as steadfastly tech-averse as ever. There are still a few remaining Australasian publications that buy his puzzles, but they're dwindling every year. He doesn't mind, though; he's paid off his mortgage and he has a small house to himself. He's doing just fine.

However, the life he chose for himself was not something my mother wanted to be a part of. After his businesses were liquidated, my father remortgaged the family house so he could support his staff, and that made my mother feel like she and us kids weren't a priority. My mum liked nice things, loved drinking a good cocktail and wanted to go out to events and parties. This no longer seemed possible to her, so she got up and left. I was eleven at the time.

She moved to a house back in Cockle Bay and my two younger sisters, Charlotte and Sophie, went with her. Soon, she had a special friend move in with her. He was an actual clown by the name of Ken Ring, who'd performed at my sister's fifth birthday, when I was ten. He was unlike anyone I had ever met in my life.

* * *

Ken Ring is a bit of an infamous name in New Zealand, and not for entirely good reasons. He gained a lot of interest in 2010 and 2011, a tumultuous time for New Zealand due to the movement of the tectonic plates beneath the country, which caused a series of devastating earthquakes in Canterbury including the deadly quake on 22 February 2011, which killed 185 people.

Ken claimed to have predicted these significant earthquakes based on the movements of the moon. Who wouldn't trust a man who spent years performing as a clown at birthday parties with that important science? Unfortunately, just enough people did trust him that he got a lot of media attention and pissed a lot of people off.

His journey of predictions began in the late 1990s, when he started publishing full-year weather reports for New Zealand, Australia and Ireland based on dubious meteorological guesses. His alternative weather predictions have seen him employed by town councils but have also been the subject of much derision.

As well as being a clown and an extreme weather forecaster, Ken has had quite the versatile career: he's taught maths, been a musician, taught English as a second language and been a magician. He was known around schools as the Mathman, the character he adopted when he went into classes to try to make mathematics fun.

He also had a book published called *Pawmistry: How to Read Your Cat's Paws*, in case you're interested in palm reading for felines. He was truly versatile (unlike most men I've dated).

I don't know the full extent of my mum and Ken's relationship, but I do know he had a house in Titirangi, way out in West Auckland. Mostly, though, he stayed in my mum's garage on the opposite side of the city from his own house.

It was an odd part of my life, that this bizarre figure from the fringes of New Zealand history played such a significant role in my upbringing. No one could have foretold it, even if they'd looked into their cat's paws, but, for all his quirks, Ken was quite an important figure for me. It was seeing him working as a clown that gave me my first aspirations to become a performer.

Seeing Ken perform magic at my sister's birthday was a pretty fundamental moment for little Nick. My sister was not entirely convinced, as she saw him hide his 'disappearing' ball and called him out on it. 'It's in your pocket, Ken!'

Despite my sister's cynicism, this performance sparked a lifelong fascination with magic for me. I love magic shows and it was Ken who inspired that in me.

While he and my mother have remained friends, the relationship never blossomed into anything beyond the walls of the garage. In fact, my mum actually came back to live with me, my brothers, Rebecca and Dad again, but things had changed.

* * *

At Four Trees, the leaky house in Howick we moved to from Cockle Bay when I was about eleven or twelve, there was a fancy second living room that my mum called the White Room. It was the nicest room in the house. There was a white sofa with matching chairs, a white shagpile rug and a big white grand piano.

There was no way in hell we, the grubby little kids, were ever allowed to set foot in that room without getting an absolute blasting. It was a place for Mum to sit, with a glass of white wine, and zone out without the noise of children.

Unfortunately for my mum, we eventually ended up running rampage in there. When Mum moved out, she took the White Room furniture with her, except for the very hard-to-move piano. Meanwhile, Dad's desire to people-please meant we got to create havoc.

With Mum gone, the White Room was up for grabs and my older brother Matthew leapt in right away to claim it. The rest of us were hugely jealous that he had the massive lounge as his bedroom. But he didn't stay there for long, thanks to my ability to bargain!

I did a little bit of work for my dad, typing up some of his crosswords so he could send them digitally. By doing that, I earnt enough to buy myself a VCR, so, for a while, I got to enjoy the thrill of watching movies in my own bedroom. That was until I realised the VCR could be used as a bargaining tool. I paired it with some CDs I knew my brother wanted, and suddenly the White Room was mine. I had secured a bedroom bigger than any other, and I loved the status it gave me.

While it didn't have the shagpile rug or the white furniture, it did have that gorgeous white piano – and I made sure to continue my mother's traditions by also never playing it. Rebecca and Matthew were much more musical than I was – my sister wrote her own music and Matthew entered Rockquest – but somehow I ended up with the beautiful instrument in my room and I didn't use it for anything except for looking at.

When my mum, who could no longer afford her own place, asked Dad if she could move back in to Four Trees (for financial rather than romantic reasons), the White Room was no longer her luxurious relaxation centre. It was now my bedroom.

Before Mum moved out, Sophie and Charlotte had always shared a room, but when they came back they each got their own bedroom because I had moved into the White Room. I think that is probably how my dad sold Mum on the news that her favourite room had been taken by me.

The whole family was back under one roof, there was no magician-slash-weather-moon-forecaster in the garage, I had the biggest room in the house all to myself ... As an optimistic young thing, I thought that maybe this was about to be the new normal. But it wasn't long before everything changed again.

* * *

Dad couldn't afford the house, so when I was around fourteen or fifteen, it had to be put on the market. We had already downgraded into this leaky home, and we had to brace ourselves to downgrade once again. It felt like we were swirling down a drain with no one there to put the plug back in.

Mum may have moved back into the house but she hadn't moved back into her marriage. It was pretty clear she wasn't happy, not least of all because she kept wandering up the street to Bill's house.

We lived right at the bottom of a cul-de-sac and Bill's place was up on the corner. He was a relatively nice man, who loved a drink in the same way that my mum did, so she would stroll up to his house in the evening and they would enjoy a bevvie together.

There wasn't anything really subtle about it. When Bill walked past our house he'd stop to ask, 'Is Bridge home?'

This wasn't just occasional either. Mum would put dinner on, wander up the street, have a drink with Bill, then have another drink with Bill … until eventually the food would be burning and we'd yell 'MUM!'

While Mum was with Bill, Rebecca would sometimes finish cooking dinner, plate it up and serve it to all of us kids. I was still too young to grasp what was really going on, but, as the house was put on the market, it was pretty clear to me that we would not all be moving together.

Once again, when she moved, my mother took her two youngest daughters with her, while me, my brothers and my older sister Rebecca stayed with Dad. Initially, Rebecca was going to leave with the other girls, but just before getting in the car she made the sudden call to stick with us. I don't know whether it was because she felt like we needed a woman around, or if she had simply lost faith in the situation, but she decided to stick with the boys.

It was a bit like when we were taught sex education at school, in that we were split up by gender so we remained completely uninformed about what half the population was going through. Dividing the family in that way was an odd decision, steeped in some kind of weird sense of traditionalism, and based on how I turned out it didn't really help maintain my masculinity. Sorry, Dad!

When I ask my parents about what happened with the money from the sale of the house we'd all lived in together, they have completely opposing replies.

'Oh no dear, I got absolutely nothing from the sale of the house. Your father absolutely pissed all the money away, sinking it into that business,' says Mum.

Dad's story differs completely as he stoically says, 'Oh look, I just gave it to Bridge because I didn't want to make a fuss.'

Whatever the case, our family had been split in two and no one felt particularly rich after it happened.

* * *

We were terrible to Bill and Mum. We hated that they would drink together, and we tried to put a stop to it.

When I was sixteen, some friends and I broke into his house, ignoring the blaring alarm, and hunted for his liquor cabinet, so we could smash it up and ruin the thing that had brought him and my mother together. We couldn't find it, so instead we ripped his phone off the wall and broke it into pieces. That way he wouldn't be able to call Mum and invite her over.

Despite our efforts, Bill and my mum stayed together for over twenty years, right until he passed away a few years ago.

I absolutely despised him when they first got together, and it stayed that way for a long time.

Bill and Mum never married, but they combined their finances and bought property together. They were each other's people. Mum was actually with him for longer than she was with Dad, so I thought it was only right that I got to know him properly.

It was hard to let Bill in. I blamed him for a lot of the distance that emerged between my mother and me, and I didn't like how much of a part alcohol played in their life together. I realise now that none of it was purely his fault, and we were such little shits whenever he was around that we deserved some of the blame for how difficult things got. Eventually, I developed something of a friendship with Bill.

I realised he was a permanent part of my family, so I started going around every few weeks, asking him questions and finding out what it was that made the man my mother loved tick. We would talk about our hopes, dreams and beliefs. His views on things like religion were pretty different from my own, but we had some good chats and he spun some pretty good yarns.

By the time Bill got sick, we had grown pretty close. He was 80, and life had suddenly caught up with him. One day, Mum came home to find him slumped in a chair, so she called an ambulance.

I spent time with him in the hospital over his last couple of days and was there for my mother as she grieved him.

I wish my siblings had been able to cross that bridge and make amends with him.

Just before he passed, he said, 'Bridget, I'm sorry. I've been a real asshole.'

I'm not sure what he was referring to. He'd also talked about seeing giant aliens on the walls around the same time, so maybe it was nothing.

Bill's kids from his first marriage came to his funeral, and it was odd. Even though my family wasn't exactly close to him, it seemed like we were more of a family to him than his own whānau. His daughter is a lesbian and hearing how impossible he found her to understand made me realise I had got it easy.

* * *

Despite all that was going on with my family, it was still the pressures of school that affected me the most. Towards the end of my time at intermediate school, I went on a school trip that turned out to be pretty damaging.

My class had all got permission slips signed and lunches packed so that we could head out to a dairy farm to find out about the beautiful world of agriculture. It certainly was not my natural habitat, but I was an optimistic young thing who would make the most out of any situation. I headed out ready to do my best and impress everyone I could.

At the farm, we were met by the old man who owned the place. He showed us around at the pace of a sleepy cow and asked us questions about farming as we walked. I don't remember what he talked about because I'm not a farmer, I don't know any facts about farming and I don't care to learn any. But I do remember how he made me feel.

When he asked a question, I raised my hand and answered it. I felt proud that I'd nailed it.

Then he responded, 'Good girl.'

The entire class erupted in laughter.

It was the most embarrassing thing I had ever experienced and I felt ill right away. It was too much to handle.

An hour or so later, he referred to me again: 'As that girl said previously ...'

I screamed on the inside. I felt lost. I was an overweight, weirdo kid with a high-pitched voice from a twice-broken home who everyone assumed was a girl. I was so scared of being called the wrong gender that I tried to double down on my more masculine traits and I purposefully tried to speak with a deeper voice ... If only that little boy could see what I do now.

As I entered high school, my family was fractured, and I was about to enter a period of unsupervised anarchy. The little goth-bogan I was always meant to be was about to arrive.

CHAPTER 3

A bogan is born

ONCE IT WAS JUST me, Matthew, Rebecca and Dad, it didn't really feel like I was living with a parent. Dad let us get away with whatever we wanted, which some might see as neglect, but it was just his way of coping. He let his kids do anything, and in many ways I did enjoy myself.

Dad didn't really like cooking, so he basically left it up to us to get our own food. This meant I spent my teenage years having the most enviable lunches at school. I had total freedom to buy whatever I wanted from the supermarket, which meant countless cans of Pringles, all the SodaStream flavours there were and a nine-pack of Cookie Time cookies in the pantry at all times. If you haven't tried a Cookie Time before, they are the most unbelievable cookie. They are the size of a pie and, even though they have more fat than a cheeseburger, they are still 100 per cent worth it. I ate them all through high school and I am still not sick of them.

My sister Sophie came over for sleepovers occasionally and every time she would freak out at the food that was available. Clearly Mum hadn't relaxed the rules the same way Dad had, so every time she arrived, she'd head straight to the pantry. Unfortunately for her, I was not into sharing.

'That's my shit! Don't you dare fucking touch it!' (Obviously, Dad was pretty loose on the rules around swearing as well.)

To this day, Sophie still talks about the food I had and how much of a dick I was not letting her have any of it. You know what? I would do it all again. I loved my delicious treats!

We did have some dinners as a family. Dad cooked very occasionally, and it was pretty much always the exact same meal: pork schnitzel and mashed potatoes. Those bags of mixed frozen vegetables also got a lot of use.

Because Dad didn't always take the lead, Rebecca continued to cook a good percentage of our meals. She ended up having to fill that mum role often, which meant keeping close tabs on me and Matthew. For her, it made life pretty difficult – part of her youth was robbed.

While we were recklessly doing whatever we wanted, she was quietly trying to keep the house together in a way that, ultimately, was too much for one young person to handle.

I wish I had understood at the time what she was going through, but I barely noticed.

The reason I barely noticed? I was running a little wild. My youth was so unsupervised that I ended up behaving in ways a teenager shouldn't. I was partying, drinking and cutting loose from far too young an age.

I should point out that I did go to school during this period. It wasn't just all partying all the time. That said, most of the time I was 'at school', I was at a place we called Waggers Hill.

Wagging, by the way, is not self-pleasure (that happened at a different hill nearby), but a term for skipping class. Depending on what part of Aotearoa you are from, you might use the terms bunking, or cutting class, but for us it was wagging. And we had a hill named after it.

I would head there pretty much every day with my three friends – and fellow garage band members – Jason, Gray and Aaron. We would be at Waggers Hill during the day, then every afternoon we would hang out in a garage, stinking up the place with Lynx Africa. I say 'garage band', because, even though we did technically have a band, we mainly just hung out in a garage, next to the instruments, drinking and listening to CDs.

We were united in our music taste, and we all loved real rock music like Metallica; Nirvana, who my older siblings had gotten me into; and my former idol, Marilyn Manson.

My friends were the straightest of straight dudes and I blended in as one of them pretty easily. I never came out to them, even after we left school, but I presume they know based on everything I've ever done since then!

They were the type of guys to hate on mainstream pop music. They viewed any song without guitar in it as shitty and fake. I kind of bought into it too. While I wasn't quite on the same level as them, I didn't have the same love for the Christinas and Britneys of the world that all the gays my age seem to love. I had loved the Spice Girls as a kid, but my newfound affection for both rock music and impressing my friends meant I never made that information public.

The incredible focus on never being 'mainstream' was hard to uphold, though. Once during our friendship, I made a potentially devastating decision: I bought an item of clothing that was actually in fashion. It was the era of Paris Hilton and Nicole Ritchie and the look that had taken over was the trucker cap.

With their netting, thick brims and Von Dutch logos, they were everywhere and I wanted one. I slipped some cash out of my dad's wallet and headed to the local market. There, in between banana fritters, I picked myself up a fake-but-fierce piece of headwear from one of the stalls. It wouldn't be the last time I felt hot wearing something fake on my head …

But when I showed up to my mate's garage with a Von Dutch hat on, my friends ripped me out. They laughed at me for trying too hard, and I succumbed to peer pressure and agreed to get rid of it. We didn't get rid of it in a normal way either. To ensure its mainstream virus never affected any of us again, we lit a fire and burnt it. As the flames licked at it, I watched on as my one attempt at being fashionable was banished forever.

My love for rock music was never about me wanting to fit in. Even though it helped me find a group of friends who could shield me from bullying, I actually really loved that music. It influenced my early drag performances in a big way. For a lot of my early gigs, I did these industrial, cybergoth looks with goggles and dreads. For Halloween one year, I performed 'Rev. 22:20' by Puscifer, which made me stand out a lot from the other queens who were doing bubblegum pop tracks. I realised quickly that it wasn't necessarily about picking a song everyone knew, but instead just using what you loved to put together the most entertaining show you could. One of the things that made me instantly stand out as a queen was the music taste I developed in those garages and while smoking cigarettes at Waggers Hill.

Waggers Hill was around the back of Howick College, and it really was the place to be when the place you didn't want to be was in class. To get there, we walked past the tennis courts and along a bush-whacked path until we arrived at the overgrown, shrubby mound of a hill. It's difficult to even call it a hill, it was just a slightly raised piece of ground – it was more like Waggers Mound … although that sounds a bit rude!

It wasn't a particularly pleasant place to spend time, but it wasn't a classroom and that was its main appeal. The path up through the bush was a bit of a maze, and a wrong turn could take you to what was essentially a huge pile of trash, so teachers were not exactly busting to get up there. It was the one place where we could bunk school and not get caught, and we would spend countless hours up there smoking the ciggies we had tricked our older siblings into buying for us.

I never got in trouble for my wagging, although one day I got extremely close. One of my mates, Aaron, was slightly less into the rock music and leaned more towards hip-hop. He was a huge fan of a group-slash-small-cult called Insane Clown Posse, who are exactly what it says on the box – insane and full of clowns. Even I, who had dreamed of being a clown, couldn't quite get into their particular brand of clownery.

Aaron was … how can I put this? … not the sharpest tool in the toolbox. He was struggling in class, and his parents were constantly frustrated by it. He didn't care. In fact, he kind of owned it. He would just tell people, 'Yeah, I'm dumb!' as if it was his identity.

Like a lot of teenagers who are not completely switched on, Aaron loved to play with fire. He constantly flicked his lighter on and off, which I guess looked kind of cool but was also an easy way to make a lighter run out of gas fast. One day up at Waggers Hill, he played a little too fast and loose with his lighter and he, either accidentally or on purpose, lit a ponga on fire. Soon enough, the plants next to the tree fern were alight and smoke was billowing up into the sky. As arresting a sight as it was, I don't think any of the staff or students at Howick College were surprised to see where the smoke was coming from. If anything at the school was going to burn down, it was the shrub-covered excuse for a hill where the slackest students hung out.

'Fuck! What do we do?' I yelled at my mates, clearly panicked by what was happening.

They looked around and shrugged. No one knew. Aaron was still just playing with his lighter as he surveyed the damage around him.

We ran back to school looking extremely guilty.

Usually, we got away with wagging because we attended enough classes that our homeroom teacher didn't suspect anything. We basically never got in trouble, which I thought was because we were so good and subtle at sneaking out.

That day, when my fat ass was running from a burning Waggers Hill, right by the perfectly positioned window of the English class I was meant to be in, I still didn't get in any trouble. It was pretty apparent from then on that no one was really keeping tabs on me – not at school and definitely not at home.

* * *

I wasn't a total write-off, though. There were certain moments when my academic side came through. It's just that I was the type of teenager who didn't think it was worth putting effort into things I had no interest in.

When I was fifteen, I had an English teacher called Ms Reilly. She was a quirky, one-of-a-kind woman who, unlike the other teachers, wasn't afraid to show us her actual, full weirdo personality. She was in her early fifties but young at heart and full of energy and warmth. She reminded me of Ms Frizzle from *The Magic School Bus* – not just because she had frizzy hair but because she was just as eccentric and kind. She was the first teacher to give me a compliment that I really valued. She was impressed by my creative writing, and the specific thing she mentioned in her feedback was my imagination: 'You write such vivid images. It's so creative, Nick. These ideas are simply marvellous.'

It was the first time in my life that I was able to see that my crazy ideas could be a good thing. I hadn't realised that being creative and having a big imagination were things people might like or that they could actually give me purpose and maybe even a career.

Ms Reilly encouraged me to do something that many other teachers actively discouraged. I'll never forget her and I hope one day I'll get my 'Adele moment' to thank her for what she gave me and for the way she helped steer me towards my destiny.

While Ms Reilly's feedback was vital, I'd actually had a glimpse of what I really wanted to do two years earlier when

I'd gone to see a whole crew of my brother's friends performing in the school show, *Jesus Christ Superstar*.

Right from the opening number, it felt like it cracked something open in me. I realised that it was actually possible to become a performer. It blew my mind. To see people who I (kind of) knew up there onstage giving it everything … I was captivated. I was looking at people that I'd seen playing PlayStation at my house with my brother, now looking like actual superstars.

As an adult, I doubt any school production is really that enjoyable to watch, but at the time I thought it was phenomenal. It is a pretty dark show filled with adult themes, it's kind of undercover quite gay (the sexual tension between Jesus and his disciples is unreal), and it features some brutal scenes like Jesus being whipped after the orders of Pontius Pilate. They didn't use an actual whip, because it's probably not cool to get high school students to whip each other, but instead they had the floggers dip their hands in red paint and then fling them so they spread red lines across the actor playing Jesus's back. My jaw was on the floor, and not just because I got to see an older guy's bare back!

There was one person in the play who immediately became my absolute idol. The boy who played Judas, who gets all of the coolest songs, was pretty much a full goth – not just on stage either, but at school as well. He had spiky hair and painted nails and he used to walk around school wearing this little girl's Care Bear backpack. I thought he was the coolest person I had ever seen. According to my older brother, he was actually a real tool. But to me, he was everything I ever wanted to be. Regardless of his personality, he wasn't afraid to dress how he wanted, when he wanted. There were no rules for him, and he looked great. Maybe he was an asshole, but he was a fierce asshole.

After seeing that musical, I knew I wanted to perform, but I couldn't quite bring myself to go through the serious intensity of being in a school production. Choreography, singing, acting ... surely I would never be able to do all that.

Instead I joined the Theatresports team. It's the only thing with 'sports' in the name that I have ever wanted to be a part of. Basically, me and the other teenagers who wanted to be on stage but who didn't want to learn lines would just play out scenes for each other. Mostly, we really just focused on trying to crack each other up.

There was a big annual Theatresports competition between all the schools in Howick, which we would plan our whole year around. No one really cared about winning the trophy, though. More important was trying to get that delicious laugh from whoever was watching.

Through Theatresports, I learnt how to improvise. It's all about listening to what your scene partner says and then adding onto it. It's about saying yes and then making more out of your partner's idea, thereby extending the scene. Before long, I became the master of flipping people's words into innuendos and gags, a skill that has since proved to be very useful indeed.

For a fat little kid who wasn't being rushed onto the sports teams or excelling in the classroom, Theatresports gave me an opportunity to both embrace myself and be whoever I wanted to be. I felt so self-conscious so much of the time, but when we were playing 'Space Jump' or 'Arms Interview' or whatever silly Theatresports game took our fancy, I got to let go and showcase a talent very few people have. It was the funnest thing I had ever done … well, until I found out about wigs.

* * *

I had my garage friends and my Theatresports friends, but the people who really shaped me were the goth girls who became a core part of every weekend.

One of my best friends in the world to this day is someone I met at the age of eleven at Sommerville Intermediate School. While this is where we first met, to be honest, it's not where we became friends.

Lisa and I first interacted at road patrol, where we were partnered together one morning a week. I don't know if road patrol exists in other countries, but here in New Zealand, children in high-vis vests are allowed to take control of pedestrian crossings by putting signs out into the street.

I wasn't usually one to sign up for extracurricular responsibilities, but I'd heard rumours that we'd get to go to Rainbow's End, which is a theme park in Auckland that was built in the 1980s, at the end of the term. In the end, we didn't even get to go there. Instead, they took us to McDonald's, which was a bit of a rough deal. Eating one Happy Meal is not quite the same as a day spent riding the Gold Rush, the Pirate Ship and the Corkscrew Coaster.

The road signs on Lisa and my friendship didn't turn to 'Go' until a few years later when the news travelled to me that Lisa was the biggest Linkin Park fan at Howick College.

'Hey, I heard you like Linkin Park.'

'Yeah, wanna come round and listen to some CDs?'

Until then, we'd never really had a proper conversation, we'd just stood opposite each other dressed in high-vis. Now, years later, we realised we actually had something in common, which led us to discover that we had many things in common.

We started hanging out, blasting Green Day, trying on different studded dog collars and experimenting with eyeliner. At the time, emo was becoming a mainstream fashion trend and Lisa and all of her friends had embraced it fully.

Slowly, I met all of her mates and, in turn, fell in love with every member of her emo coven. They were as close to goths as they could be on a teenager's budget. Lisa's hair was bright pink and her friend Gemma had dyed hers black with red streaks. Meanwhile, I bought myself the longest trench coat

I could find, shaved my hair into a mohawk and, together, we were ready to paint the town black.

'Grafton this weekend?' was a question that was asked every single week, and we all knew exactly what it meant.

Every weekend, we would head to the most gothic place we could imagine: Symonds Street Cemetery, on the corner of Karangahape Road and Symonds Street.

It's a long way from Howick to central Auckland, and our parents would never have been okay with dropping us off at a graveyard, so we usually hitchhiked into the city.

Melissa, with her thick dreadlocks in pigtails, and Erin, whose sleek black hair ran all the way down her back, would stand at the side of the road with their thumbs out, waiting for some horny guy on his way into town to pick us up. Classy as ever, I would hide in a nearby bush.

Just as the car pulled over, I would emerge from my leafy hiding place and jump in the back seat.

'Hiiiiiiii! Thanks for the ride!' (Surprise – you got a fatty too!)

In my giant trench coat with my pink spiky hair and my high-pitched voice, I doubt many of them even realised I was a boy. What I am certain of is that not one of them was ever stoked to have me in their car.

Once we made it to town, we would spend the night at the cemetery, drinking the cheapest booze we could get our teenage hands on and talking to whichever shady strangers came our way. It was a dodgy part of town and, given the legal age for buying alcohol in New Zealand was eighteen, we were too young to be drinking, but the place became a staple part of our lives.

All sorts of goths from across the city came to hang out in a relatively small park surrounded by dead people. It was not many people's idea of a dream Saturday night, but we loved it.

The lack of supervision from my dad meant I never once got in trouble for heading there either. For all I know, he might be reading this right now and only just realising where I used to spend my Saturday nights.

At the end of the night, when we were all gothed out and ready to scoop ourselves up and take ourselves home, we would scrabble together the $6 we needed to catch the 3 am NiteRider bus back to Howick. In the – let's be honest, quite likely – event that we didn't get organised in time to catch the bus, we would badger our friend Chloe until she eventually caved in and called her mum.

'Mum, we're absolutely stranded in town and we need your help!'

The poor woman was left with no choice but to make the 30-minute drive into town at four in the morning to pick up her daughter and her daughter's goth mates.

A few times, I didn't even make it back to my own house. Instead, I would finish drinking my cask wine on the school campus, and then I would inflate the empty goon sack, emptying my lungs into its shiny silver chamber, then use it as my pillow as I slept the night on the bleachers outside the Howick College common room. In the morning, I'd wake up and go straight to class, or, if I didn't feel like school, I'd just go home. Sleeping on an inflated empty goon sack? I'm a bogan icon, no matter how badly my bogan look went down on *Drag Race*!

Eventually, my dear pal Lisa achieved something extremely rare. In fact, she is the only person in the world to have ever done it. Lisa became my girlfriend.

We were drinking at Lloyd Elsmore Park one night, and the inspiration took me. I had been thinking about it for a while, caught up in societal expectations that I should start dating a girl, and because Lisa and I were both overweight and emo, I figured that was all we needed, that we were a perfect match.

That night in the park, I quickly, privately surveyed each of our friends one by one, having the same conversation again and again.

'I'm thinking of asking Lisa out …'

'Oh my god! You should totally ask Lisa out!'

'I'm gonna do it!'

All of our friends became our own little audience as I approached Lisa. They giggled as we started talking. They were all staring at us, like giddy little children, so Lisa could tell something was up.

'Why is everyone laughing at us?' she asked.

'Nick's got a question for you!' they jibed her. We were almost eighteen but they were acting like we were children in a playground.

I built up the courage to ask her. 'Lisa, do you wanna like … be my girlfriend? Or whatever …'

My lack of conviction probably gave away that a girlfriend was not something I actually wanted, but that didn't matter to Lisa.

She replied instantly, 'Yeah, keen as.'

The relationship was short. Like, super duper short. Danny DeVito short. We probably didn't even go on what would constitute a real date before I suddenly changed my tune.

'Hey, I think we might be better as friends.'

Lisa was confused and quite upset, and that is fair enough. It would be a while before I could admit the proper reason – that I was a total poof – but, luckily, we were able to remain friends.

Her and her gorgeous gothy mates would come to what me and my guy friends referred to as 'parties', even though they really were just beers in the garage. We would hang out in my friend Gray's garage and muck around listening to rock music and drinking cans of bourbon and coke, which had such a high alcohol percentage that they are illegal now.

We were united not just by what we loved but also by how popular we were. We sat in that perfect middle ground – we weren't the 'cool kids', but we weren't noticeable enough for people to make fun of us. We were invisible to most of the school, and that suited me just fine because being a queer teenager in the early 2000s did not look that fun.

In all my time at school, I only ever saw one other gay kid. I say 'saw' because I definitely did not ever talk to him. His name was Craig and, while we never spoke at school, we have connected online since then and briefly talked about our very different queer experiences of Howick College.

We had mutual friends, but we never hung out with each other. This was probably because, despite the huge thing we had in common, we were quite different. While I did my best to blend in, branding myself strongly as a goth and hanging out with a gang of straight boys, Craig was out, femme and so tall there was no way for him to avoid the attention of the whole school.

Craig was a giant, not just tall but with long, loose limbs, which gesticulated as he talked in a way that meant his flamboyance could be spotted from halfway across the field. He fully embraced his feminine side, even wearing the girls' uniform to school. On one level, I was jealous that he was so openly able to accept exactly who he was, but mostly I saw how he was treated by other students and I knew I did *not* want that.

I didn't feel any malice or dislike for Craig, but, because he stood out so much, he quickly became the object of hateful behaviour. He was the butt of so many jokes, and I never called anyone out for making those jokes. Inside, I knew that

I was definitely gay, but I was not brave enough to tell anyone and I certainly didn't feel brave enough to stand up for Craig. I certainly didn't want to exhibit the feminine traits that he did, although – amazingly – I am now a drag queen and he has grown up to be a much more masculine gay man.

I knew that if anyone found out about my little secret, I would become the butt of jokes just like he was, so I buried it as deep as I could. It wasn't getting out, not until I got out of Howick.

CHAPTER 4

Gay Lynn

IT TOOK ME A couple of attempts to leave school. Like anal sex, the first time can sometimes be messy. I left at the start of sixth form (Year 12) and was sure I would be all independent and out on my own, living my dream life. In reality, I was lazy and I basically sat on my butt for six months. Obviously, I'm an ambitious person who gets things done – you have to be driven to pursue a career in drag and keep at it – but the truth is, hiding behind that hard-working persona is a much lazier version of myself, who is desperate to escape. I let him out after I dropped out of school, but ever since then I've done my best to keep him locked away.

Everything was better when I went back to school for my final year. I was a seventh former doing sixth-form subjects, I didn't have to wear a uniform, so I felt a bit more grown-up, and I had the chance to finish my subjects and get what I needed to enter the big wide world. I only studied part-time, which meant I didn't feel the need to hang out in the burnt-up remains of Waggers Hill as I had plenty of free time. Drama was my favourite subject and I was stoked to be able to get back to it, especially as they let me skip sixth form and join the seventh form class.

After I got the qualifications I needed and was able to leave school, I took another not-so-brief break, which I spent sitting around. I then made a very informed and respectable decision about my future life and career – instead of figuring out what I actually wanted to do with my life, I decided to study the exact same thing that my brother was studying. So, my porky eighteen-year-old ass enrolled myself in chef's school. Mainly, I did it because I thought there might be lots of delicious treats I would get to eat for free. I did get to eat many things, but it definitely didn't feel like I was getting them for free.

Despite picking the course just because it seemed like the easy option at the time, once I had enrolled, I grew to love cooking – and to this day, I still do. It was everything else about the course that I found a bit harder to swallow.

What I thought would be a chill, easy few years of cooking some food and then chowing down on it was actually an impossibly hard, incredibly stressful nightmare where I heard some of the worst things I have ever heard come out of another human's mouth.

As the saying goes, if you don't like the heat, get out of the kitchen, and the heat was definitely too much for me. The tutor was, to put it mildly, the biggest fucking asshole I have ever met in my life. He was a monster who thrived on yelling at his pupils and telling us how bad we were at what we were doing.

Just cooking at the school was tough enough, but eventually we had to go into an operating kitchen at a restaurant, and it was there that things were taken to the next level. I genuinely tried so hard. I wanted to be good at it, but clearly my best was not enough. The tutor walked up to a dish I had plated and, out of nowhere, just went ballistic at me. It seemed as if he was getting off on it.

'What the hell are you thinking? This isn't the '80s! You can't garnish a dish with parsley!'

It was tough enough that he was coming for my work, but pretty soon he started criticising who I was as a person. It was brutal.

'You're never going to be a chef at this rate, faggot.'

I had been called that awful word before, for sure, but usually from a Nissan Skyline as it drove past. This was the first time that an authority figure had decided to call me that, and this was years before I had even come to terms with my own identity. I had to leave.

It was so tense and stressful, but I'm also a messy bitch who loves drama, so walking out felt pretty delicious.

From then on I realised it wasn't worth doing something because I felt like I should, because it seemed like what I should be doing. I wanted to find something to do with my life that brought me joy. What would that be? It was going to be a while before I figured it out.

At nineteen, having given up on my course and a career in food, I headed out into the big wide world and got a job … with my mum.

Mum was working as a caregiver for people with disability and my sister was working with her, and so I jumped in too. I also decided I needed to spend some time *not* in the vicinity of members of my family, so I moved out of my dad's place and into a flat in sunny Grey Lynn.

The central Auckland suburb of Grey Lynn used to be an amazing, vibrant community of mainly Māori and Pacific Islanders, who populated the gorgeous, rundown villas that dominate the suburb. In the 2000s, however, it was visited by that old queen Jen Trafication and now it's truly the home to the richest-of-the-rich, having been taken over by wealthy white people, who pay $2 million for uninsulated properties with 'character'. There are lots of places with good coffee now, though.

I got there just as this change was beginning, when renting there was still vaguely affordable. It was in my Grey Lynn flat that I would meet some of the most important people in my entire life, including my best guy friend, Karl.

Karl is a completely straight guy who has been an incredible friend to me over the years. He is loyal, compassionate and a lot of fun. He marches to the beat of his own drum at all times in a way I cannot help but love. He works as a builder, but he's also an artist, and his desire to create art permeates every facet of his life.

In Grey Lynn, he did paintings on our walls, and he upcycled rubbish into freaky little art pieces to decorate the lounge. In the hallway between our bedrooms, we made what we called the 'buzz room' with chicken-wire mesh cable-tied to a kid's toy lawnmower to make the strangest little art pieces you can imagine.

Karl had 28-millimetre ear stretchers and tattoos everywhere. On his days off, he would wear what he called his 'baggy sack', which was just a duvet cover he'd cut arm and leg holes into, and he would walk around the house completely naked but for this duvet cover. When the baggy sack was on, it was time to get out what we called TPs, short for 'Twelve Percenters', which were drinks with – you guessed it – 12 per cent alcohol that we used to absolutely go nuts on. They were some of the greatest times of my life.

Living together was perfect. Karl and I were totally compatible and always ready to hang out. We would work our jobs, then drink every time we had a day off. Together, we tried magic mushrooms, ecstasy and acid for the first time, really getting a bit of a drug education they don't give you at school.

This was during the brief time when party pills, known to people who didn't do them as BZPs, were available legally in New Zealand. These were basically pills that would hit you as hard as any drug and would keep you up and going for a whole night. They were intense, but you had to take heaps of them to get a good high.

At the time, New Zealand was the only country to have them legally on the market, thanks to self-proclaimed 'party king' Matt Bowden, who convinced the government that BZPs were a potential tool to help get people off methamphetamine. As a result, for a period, anyone of any age could purchase any dose from many local shops. Unfortunately for Matt, and a whole bunch of the people who took them, BZPs came with some extremely adverse side-effects, including toxic shock and psychosis. Eventually, in 2008, they were made illegal.

We were lucky enough to have enjoyed them without the toxic side effects, and, for the years I was living in that Grey Lynn flat, I partied hard on pills and Scrumpy apple cider as I got closer and closer to my new best mate.

Karl is effervescent. He is the life of the party, the sort of person everyone wants to be friends with. He is always chill – the king of relaxing – and never takes things personally, but he's also a total goofball and will fully commit to any kind of silliness that happens.

I basically fell in love with him, and even though I had a sneaking suspicion he knew about my feelings, we never spoke about it, and he remained my best friend and I knew he would stick by me no matter what my future held.

Those partying days were responsible for a pretty delightful scar that led me to give up drugs entirely. We were high as anything on ecstasy, partying like mad. Karl had this builders' craft knife that was super, terrifyingly sharp.

Absolutely pilling out, I picked up the knife.

'What if I cut my hand with this?' I asked Karl.

'Please don't do that. Really, don't,' he replied, his high replaced by adrenaline-fuelled safety concerns.

I didn't listen. I brought the craft knife down to my hand, and by simply doing what felt like holding it over the back of my hand, I popped the flesh open into a huge gaping wound. It was raw, disgusting and, for some reason, hilarious to me. We tried to tape it back together with Sellotape, but it kept bursting.

The one sober person at the party drove us to the hospital, and a nurse sewed it back together as I kept laughing at what was going on. I kept calling it my handgina and comparing it to a vagina like the stupid little gay boy I was.

As soon as the stitches were finished, reality came crashing in: I realised how stupid I had been and decided that might be it for me and drugs.

This did, however, come with one surprise bonus. Because I was working as a caregiver for elderly people, I couldn't really turn up to work with a gaping wound on my hand ready to be infected, so I got a whole heap of time off.

Living in the flat with Karl and me was a guy called Sean, who was a friend of my high-school garage mates. It was actually through them that I'd met Sean and subsequently moved in with him.

Sean's girlfriend eventually moved in with us as well. When you're young and want more money to spend on party pills, having someone's partner move in to reduce the rent is something you say yes to instantly. Unfortunately, Sean's girlfriend didn't save us much money. In fact, she did quite the opposite.

One day, our landlord turned up without warning, demanding to know where the rent was. We had, in a move that was maybe a bit sexist, decided to put Sean's girlfriend in charge of collecting and paying the rent. It turned out that after everyone gave her all that rent money and she'd seen it in her account, she hadn't wanted to give it away. For over a month, she hadn't paid any rent, so we got kicked out, and I ended up back in my dad's garage.

I spent a sad few months in the garage, but it was a good chance to save up so I could party hard when we eventually got the flat back together. It turned out we didn't end up back in just any flat together, we ended up back in the very same flat.

The landlord was a colleague of Karl's, so Karl made sure to turn up the charm every time he saw him on a job. Eventually, he agreed to let us move back into the house, but this time without Sean and his charming lady. Replacing Sean was my dear friend Lisa.

Lisa and I had moved on from protecting the road outside our school as twelve-year-olds to taking pills together every weekend as twenty-year-olds. We still loved dressing up in the same goth stuff we wore at high school, and we still blasted Linkin Park from the giant boombox in our lounge. We had always been bogans but now we were old enough to live that life full-time.

During this time, my friend Quentin got me a pretty iconic part-time job. He had been friends with Jason and my other garage friends, but had always been slightly geeky and a bit on the outside of the group. He was a great person to have around, though, as he was always happy to get us a tinny or sober drive for us.

Being the amazing, helpful friend that he was, Quentin hooked me up with a job most young New Zealanders dream of – controlling the rides at Rainbow's End. Who wouldn't want to work at New Zealand's only theme park, the funnest place in South Auckland (not a hard thing to achieve back then)?

Initially, I was stoked to get the job, and I definitely felt powerful operating all those important switches that made the go-karts head down the tracks. One day, though, the job lost its fun for me.

We had to wear a Rainbow's End uniform, but they didn't have one that fitted me. Instead, I was given highlighter-blue shorts and an awful shirt that were both too small for me. When I was working on the Bumper Boats for the first time,

I bent down to help a kid out of a boat and … *rrrrrippp!* The shorts split right down my ass.

I didn't know what to do, so I ran. I ran like I had never run in my life. I ran out of the theme park, into the carpark and across to my car, then I jumped into it and sped home. A week later, I did a drive-by of the entrance and chucked a plastic bag with my uniform in it out the window of the car to make sure they knew I was done. I never went back. My employment at Rainbow's End lasted for exactly one week of the school holidays.

Quentin quit soon after I did, and when he did, he saved a costume of one of the Rainbow's End characters from the skip bin and brought it back to our Grey Lynn flat. For years, we had this amazing fibreglass parrot head, which we would add lights to and go crazy with at our parties. The parrot costume also came with these amazing fluorescent green, furry pants, which Karl cut into the most fabulous pants for himself.

Lisa, Karl and I loved hosting parties, and we had a big group of mates who would come over every other weekend. Eventually we thought, why not keep this party vibe going at all times?

Our small, three-person Grey Lynn flat mutated into an eleven-person gaggle living in a six-bedroom house in Avondale in Auckland's inner west. We had couples living in the garage and people sharing rooms. On big party nights, we even dragged our mattresses out into the garden so we could spin out under the stars.

We once dug an enormous hole in the front lawn and placed a pot inside it, then we used a massive roll of black polyurethane to build a fort around the hole. That night, we sat around the fort lighting all sorts of fireworks (most of which are now illegal in New Zealand). Lying on our mattresses, we looked up at the sky and watched the fireworks explode. It felt perfect.

It was in that house in Avondale that I would try drag for the first time, come out for the first time and just generally have some of the best times of my life. I went in as Nick, but during this phase of my life I evolved into Kita.

* * *

As well as getting me a job at Rainbow's End, Quentin was also part of an amazing band I was in called Whorgy. We were a trio of rockers who put out music with some truly crass lyrics. You won't find any of our songs online these days because I recently found them and deleted them in shame!

Our singer was my friend Zanny, who is a legendary party queen. She came to her first Grey Lynn party when she was fifteen, and even though she was way too young to be there, she was a good time so we kept inviting her. She had an incredible, intense presence, which gave her just the right amount of big dick energy to be a great lead singer. Quentin wrote her the most ruthless sexual lyrics about masturbation, degradation and ejaculation among (many) other things, which she really knew how to sell.

It wasn't just our lyrics that were controversial – we made sure to rebel in the way we dressed as well. Zanny and I would dress up freaky and perform like we were demonic, horny monsters. For Halloween gigs, we would wear Christmas outfits. At Christmas, we would dress as Easter bunnies. We would do everything we could to subvert the norms, and we thought we were so cool while we did it. We might not have always sounded great, but we always made a big impression.

At first I played the drums, but when we lost our bassist I made the jump to bass guitar (which I didn't know how to play ... not even a little bit). I would pre-programme the drum machine so that I could just press play then focus on my terrible bass playing.

We did quite a few gigs and slowly built up what I guess you could call a cult (read: small) following. Our fans loved us, though, and someone must have particularly loved us because we eventually got hired to do a gig in a sex dungeon at some type of swingers' party.

'You guys will go down a treat!'

'I don't think we will be the biggest treat on the menu ...'

We were lucky that no one was having sex in the room we were playing in, at least as far as we could see.

I'd just started dabbling in a little bit of drag, so I performed in a kind of androgynous draggy look, with a corset and my man-nips hanging out. It was a look that I thought would really make an impression on the crowd, but they weren't really paying attention to the band onstage. They had other stuff to do.

Eventually Zanny and Quentin started fighting and they got to a point where they couldn't work together. Zanny wanted to keep performing without Quentin, but he rightfully pointed out that he had written all of the lyrics to our songs so they were kind of his.

You're probably thinking, 'Damn, I wish that band would get back together so I could enjoy this musical artistry live,' but unfortunately we will not be touring any time soon. Maybe someday we will find the motivation to do it, but for now we are going to have to keep our fans waiting.

* * *

You might have the impression that I'm a real softy and that I would never do anything wrong. But that's only half right. I *am* a softy, but I have definitely done the wrong thing on occasion. Some of them were totally my fault, while at other times I like to think I was on the right side of history.

New Zealand still hasn't legalised weed, despite a referendum in 2020 that got tantalisingly close. Even so, it's not too often that you hear of people getting arrested for using it. Well, people, I'm here to tell you it does happen.

I was twenty, parked up in a car, enjoying a nice joint, when a big police wagon pulled up behind me. Even back then, the police didn't arrest many people for smoking marijuana, but I think they saw me with my weird blue hair, studs and big leather trench coat and wanted to make an example of me.

They drove me around in their wagon for hours. They had found this young goth kid doing something harmless but technically illegal, and they wanted to give me a scare so they drove around hoping to arrest some more – possibly scarier – people who I would end up stuck in the back of the police wagon with. Alas, they couldn't find anyone else to arrest so they drove me back to the station.

The cops were definitely assholes. As I was being processed at the station, they kept making fun of me, mocking my Smurf hair, my studs, my weight and taking sneaky photos of me on their phones. Who knows where those photos were being sent? I lost a lot of respect for the police force that day.

On other occasions that I got in trouble with the police, I deserved it. Issues with drinking ran in my family, and while I have sorted myself now, when I was fresh out of high school I made some big mistakes.

When I first started drinking, I wasn't the best at regulating how much alcohol I had consumed. I first got done for drink-driving when I was seventeen. Because I was under eighteen and didn't have a full licence yet, I ended up having to pay a fine and do some community service. For community service, I worked doing random odd jobs and helping pack food parcels at the Salvation Army, but when that got a bit too exhausting I charmed the pants off the person supervising me and got transferred to a marae where they let me just bum around. I shouldn't have got off so easy, but I did.

A couple of years later, I got done again and got disqualified from driving. Then I drove while I was disqualified. When you drive while you are disqualified and get pulled over, they do the full shebang. You get properly, publicly arrested. They make a spectacle of you on the street, then they tow your car away and lock it up.

I ended up in front of a judge who basically told me that if he saw me in his court again he would come down hard and I wouldn't be able to drive for a long time. That was a pretty good wake-up call. It was time to stop breaking the road rules and focus on breaking the gender rules instead. After all, one of those costs money and risks lives, and the other can make you money and save your life.

If I'd been a more superstitious man, I might have decided to get rid of my car, as it was in that little shitbox Toyota Corsa – which I was still, very slowly, paying off on finance – that I often found myself in the worst spots.

A few years after my day in court, I was driving my friend Tabitha's sister Sam down Dominion Road. (A little tip: if you are ever in Tāmaki Makaurau/Auckland and want good dumplings, Dominion Road is where you want to head. But that's neither here nor there.)

On our way home, I decided to shout Sam some McDonald's. With our order on board, I turned out of the drive-thru the wrong way, so I tried to do a U-turn as quickly as I could. As I turned around, a car pulled up behind me and T-boned us, blocking us into a side street. I saw three guys get out of the car and walk towards us.

The last thing I remember before I woke up, covered in blood on the side of the road, was those men dragging Sam and me out of my car. They'd beaten the shit out of me, Sam had been attacked too and the car was gone.

Sam and I stumbled to a petrol station a couple of blocks away where we called the police. They were much friendlier to me than they had been when they caught me smoking weed. They asked all sorts of questions about what we remembered about what had happened, what the men looked like, what they'd been driving and what else had been in my car.

One thing that had been in the car was my little Dickies satchel. Even though I wasn't fully out at the time, I had already started carrying what was essentially a – slightly less femme – handbag. It went with me everywhere, and in it were my cigarettes, my lighter, my wallet, my Sanyo Pinkalicious flip-phone … all the essentials!

Later that night, the police questioned a group of five guys, one of whom had my Dickies bag. You see – it pays to carry a bag, boys!

My car was found burnt out, and the guys went to court. I had to go and give evidence against them, but the police talked me into helping them focus all the charges on just one member of the group. He went to prison and I ended up getting some reparations to cover my destroyed property – among which was a pair of heels I had borrowed from my friend Eli. I'd been taking them out for a casual test-run as I started to explore the idea of drag.

CHAPTER 5

Dragging things out

L ong before there was Kita, there was Petra. If anyone thinks I got into drag to be pretty, one photo of this beast of a woman will prove that that was not my intention.

It all started with a classic round of Secret Santa. One of my housemates got me one of my most favourite gifts: a megaphone. I don't know what made them look at me – the loudest, most camp, most obnoxious person in the house – and think, 'Let's make that voice even louder!', but I loved it and couldn't stop using it.

What I loved most about this particular megaphone was that it didn't just make my voice louder, but it could also distort it. I guess I have a burning desire to be as irritating as possible, because I took this tool and used it to make my voice piercingly high.

From that annoying voice, I gave birth to the terrifying Petra, who would hide around corners and scream, 'Oh my gawwwwwwwwwd!' when my flatties were least expecting it. Imagine Janice from *Friends* turned up to eleven and hiding in your kitchen when you go to get a snack – that was Petra.

After annoying my flatmates with the megaphone for weeks, I decided Petra needed a look for our New Year's Eve party.

Some people might think that putting together a drag look involves sketching a perfect vision then either sewing it yourself or handing it over to a designer to make your dreams come true. Let's be honest, 99.99 per cent of drag is not like that at all. Instead, it's about begging, borrowing and stealing from your friends so you can put together something that hopefully looks okay.

For Petra, it started with a skirt. Not just any skirt, a high-school formal dress skirt. My sister Rebecca had made a metallic burgundy top and skirt for her senior ball, and, while it wasn't the exact colour I wanted, it made up for that in one crucial way: it fitted me.

What did my sister think of me stealing her prized ball outfit?

She didn't know … and she still doesn't. I've never told her I took it.

It would have been easier if I had taken the whole outfit, but as I looked at it, I thought the same thing I've thought many times when I've been on Grindr: this top just isn't going to work for me.

To find a top that I might actually be able to get on my body, I enlisted the help of my flatmate Lisa. What a delightful treat for her to have her ex-boyfriend ask if he could borrow some of her most feminine clothes.

To match the metallic burgundy skirt, Lisa provided me with a matte-metallic, leopard-print top that, luckily for me, was extremely stretchy. Trust me, it clashed even worse than what anyone who didn't see it could imagine. That didn't matter for the character I was creating. Clashing patterns were not a concern for Petra.

With her clothing sorted, the look wasn't going to be complete until Petra had some hair. I went to the local party store and stepped into the wig aisle, which was populated by some of the cheapest and most flammable excuses for hairpieces ever created. One in particular called my name. It had some kind of generic name like 'Fun Blonde' and it was a mop of long, messy, noodle-like blonde curls. It was then that I realised Petra's style icon was absolutely Miss Piggy.

Luckily, I had a spare few dollars to buy what would complete the look: a pig snout to strap to my face.

New Year's Eve arrived and Lisa helped me into the outfit. It was an abomination.

'You look a mess,' said Lisa.

She was right. And I loved it.

With no heels, no make-up and no filter, I roamed around the dance floor acting even more of a mess than I looked and using my megaphone to annoy the shit out of my friends.

So my first time in drag was a bit of a shambles. The only tip I got from my audience was a light suggestion to tone it down, but that didn't stop me. I loved inhabiting my creation and showing off in front of my friends.

Petra ruled the party and I felt on top of the world. In my pig snout, my leopard print, my noodle hair and my sister's skirt, I felt like a queen. It was probably time I told people I was gay.

* * *

Yes, I'd been wearing dresses since I'd been in nappies, but I still actually had to *tell* people I was one of those homosexuals they had heard so much about. For a lot of people, coming out is a torturous, long process. For me, it was just one of many nights I'd spent drinking and shooting the shit with Karl when the rest of the flat had gone to bed.

Out of nowhere he said to me, 'So, you're gay right?'

Almost as if it was nothing, I replied, 'Oh, yeah.'

And then it was done. Karl told me how fine that was and that I didn't have to worry.

Telling the rest of the flat, however, was slightly more dramatic.

One of my flatmates, Tabitha, and I used to get into fights. We would storm around the flat, yelling at each other over the most menial issues. We had one particularly intense screaming match over dishes being left next to the sink, which led to us both going off in a huff to our rooms.

An hour passed before she came to my room with an apology. 'I'm sorry, Nick. The reason I got so angry is that, well, I have a crush on you.'

It was not what I was expecting, to say the least. For *anyone* to have a crush on me was a shock. At that point, I was so fucking fat, I had the strangest haircut and I did weird shit all the time. (Petra was just one of the many annoying characters I did around the house.) Surely no one could fall in love with that? In many ways, I was flattered, but I also felt extremely awkward.

Luckily, I had a pretty good way to end the conversation.

'Thank you, but I'm gay. I'm so fucking gay.'

Tabitha is now a mother, so I think she must have eventually got over that crush!

As my most loud-mouthed friend, though, she told everyone in the house, and soon all of my friends knew. The news even somehow leaked to my sister.

I was working with Rebecca in one of my many side jobs selling newspaper subscriptions over the phone. She must have heard the gossip around the office because one day she swivelled her chair around and decided to drop a bombshell on me.

'Carolyn said she heard you're gay.'

'What?'

'She was talking to her friend Greg, and he said he knew you and that you were gay. Don't worry, I put her in her place. "Come on, Carolyn. I think I'd know if my brother was gay."'

Oh well, might as well rip the Band-Aid off and get it over with.

'Well, what if I am?'

'Are you gay?'

'I am.'

She was shocked to have been left in the dark and wanted to know why I hadn't told her sooner. I actually knew the answer to that question.

Years earlier, there had been some news story on TV about gay people. I can't remember what the story was about but it was in the late 1990s, years before marriage equality, so it's likely it wasn't a positive one.

While the story played, my sister turned to my dad and said, 'There's no homosexuals in our family, are there, Dad?'

'Of course not, sweetie,' was his reply.

I couldn't help but feel that her question had been directed at me. I felt she wasn't actually asking if we had any gay people in the whānau, but that she was telling me – in a roundabout way – that I was not allowed to be gay. She swears this never happened, but I remember it so vividly. It just goes to show that just one flippant thing you say can live with another person for years.

I let Rebecca spread the news to the rest of the family as I couldn't be bothered having that conversation multiple times.

Mum rang me a few weeks later.

'I'm calling because I think there might be something to tell me?'

'Um, no, not really.'

I didn't let her have the big coming-out conversation because I just didn't really think we should need to. *This is who I am. We don't need a big chat to break that down.*

Soon everyone knew, which was great, because another New Year's party was coming up and I wanted to wear a dress again.

* * *

When I say I wanted to wear a dress, that doesn't mean I wanted to be pretty. Almost the opposite was true. This time I wanted to go full clown.

My friends Gemma and Richard were hosting a party and the theme of the party was 'Famous'. I wanted to go as the most famous person there has ever been – no, not Jesus … Ronald McDonald. I figured with all the money I'd given the institution of McDonald's over the years, I'd pretty much bought the rights to use their mascot's image for the evening.

This time, I wanted to level up the look. I wanted to go all out. Unfortunately, I still didn't have the coin or the knowledge to purchase or make anything that was even close to being glamorous. What I did have, however, was a beanbag. Well, technically, it belonged to my niece.

My half-brother Craig had been about to throw out his daughter's Barbie beanbag because it was covered in mould. When I looked at it, I didn't see the mould-covered face of America's favourite doll. I saw potential for a dress that might actually fit me. The tapered shape, the volume at the bottom – all she needed was a neck hole, some armholes, and a hole at the bottom for my feet and she'd be ready to wear.

I saved the sack from its trip to the rubbish bin and got to work. I washed it, and I got rid of most of the mould. Well, some of the mould. Truthfully, a little bit of the mould. It was quite stubborn, but I wasn't going to let some health risk get in the way of my look.

I dyed the beanbag yellow, painted on the Golden Arches, cinched it with a belt, sewed a hula hoop in the bottom to give it some shape, found some bright red-and-white tights and did my first ever wig styling on a Two Dollar Shop red wig. I styled it into a hair-bow similar to the ones Lady Gaga was wearing at the time – at least, as close to that as I could get. I modelled my make-up after the only drag queens I'd seen on TV at that point. With super high brows and huge red lips, I went full clown. It was certainly a look that made an impression.

At a party full of people dressed as Paris Hilton, Lindsay Lohan and the sexy blue people from *Avatar*, it was hard to miss me: the enormous man in a dress made of furniture covering. If people think the clown from *It* was scary, this creation would send them over the edge. If my version of Ronald became the ambassador for McDonald's, I reckon I could put the most popular burger company in the world out of business!

Busted as I may have looked, my friends could tell that I had discovered something that had awakened a real passion in me. I didn't know what to do with that passion, but luckily a few of them had an idea.

* * *

Whenever I took on a new drag character, I thrived, and my friends took notice. Without my knowledge, Tabitha signed me up for a drag competition. I'd never even mentioned the idea to her, but she showed me the flyer and the conversation went something like this:

'You're doing this.'

'I …'

'You're doing this.'

At that point, I had no idea what it even really meant to be a drag queen, but I knew I needed to elevate my looks … literally. I needed to buy my first pair of heels.

I had no idea of the many wondrous shops that sell large shoes designed specifically for cross-dressers, so instead I went to the weird and wonderful world of Trade Me. It is New Zealand's version of eBay and the place where I've found many of my most prized drag accessories. There, I hit the jackpot with a pair of size 11 satin kitten heels that reached the lofty heights of approximately one inch!

I borrowed a few items from Lisa, taped on a blonde wig, which had also come from the hidden corners of Trade Me, and wrapped myself in a hideous cream-coloured woollen shawl that for some reason made me feel like the very definition of a woman.

The show was happening at Galatos, a rough and ready music venue that has also been the home of some iconic parties, just off Aotearoa's queerest street, Karangahape Road. At this point, I'd pretty much never been out clubbing before and had definitely never set foot in a gay club, which meant I'd never seen a drag show.

As we approached the venue, it suddenly hit me: I had no idea what a drag queen was supposed to do. I knew they were out there and I knew they wore fabulous outfits, but I didn't know what they *did* at clubs, so I turned up to my first drag show with no concept of what was in store. For all I knew, I might have been expected to walk on a tightrope or fight a tiger.

As we turned off Karangahape Road, I started to get nervous. We were heading down a back alley, there was barely anyone around and the few people that were seemed like they might be looking for a fight. We walked up to the door of Galatos and I took a deep breath: whatever this night required of me, I was ready to give it my all.

But when we opened the door … it was empty. No one was there.

A bemused bartender looked me up and down.

'I'm here for the drag competition,' I announced.

'I'm sorry, sweetheart, that event was cancelled due to lack of interest.'

I looked at my friends, gutted. I looked down at what I was wearing and it suddenly felt so silly. A drag queen always stands out in a room, but when that room isn't expecting a drag queen, and the one that shows up is looking busted as hell, she stands out even more.

Even so, I couldn't let this outfit (if you could call it that) go to waste. I had never been to a gay bar, but I knew we were just around the corner from Family Bar, the most famous gay bar in the country. This night was not going to end in tragedy – I could still be the queen I had come all the way from Avondale to be!

We walked into Family Bar and I got noticed immediately. I mean, it was hard to miss me. I was enormous, terrified and wearing a shawl in a nightclub. These one-inch heels, which I could barely keep my balance on, were giving me serious height. I could feel the people around me staring, and I knew I liked the feeling.

My friends and I were having a great night, dancing, chatting, drinking more tequila than we should have. I had no idea that this night was about to change my life forever because someone extremely famous and important was there.

A piercingly loud voice carried across the club. 'Look at you, girl!'

I looked across the bar and saw an actual, real-life celebrity. I didn't know much about the New Zealand drag scene, but there was one queen I *did* know about. She'd even been on TV. For the sake of the story, we'll call her Peena Colada.

'Come chat, sis!' she said.

She brought me outside to the front courtyard, and I was instantly spellbound. I'd never seen anyone with the kind of effortless confidence she seemed to have. Drinks were brought over without her even asking. Whenever anyone entered, she greeted them by name, and they seemed thrilled to see her. She had that star power that made everyone around her feel special. She made me feel special.

On this night, which had begun with me feeling like the most unimportant, useless piece of trash, dressed in a bunch of rags and turned away from a cancelled gig, quickly became the night everything changed for me – she was my hero. I got butterflies every time she talked. I couldn't get over the fact that she had noticed me, and I couldn't believe how amazing she was.

She was hilarious, welcoming and so much fun. I'd never met anyone so sassy and so gay. I knew almost no gay people at this point, so to see someone be so fearlessly gay was hypnotising. She commanded the space around her; everyone listening to her stories and hearing her shady calls was enraptured. She was magnetic and I couldn't take my eyes off her.

She must have liked something about me too because she invited me to another event, which would become my true first drag performance.

'Come back here next Friday, ask for me. Wear something better than that. Those heels are about three inches too short!'

I couldn't believe she'd cared to talk to me, and that I'd already booked a gig, but Peena had seen something in me. It was all about to happen.

* * *

'Peena Colada would like to see you in the drag room.'

This was simultaneously the most terrifying and most exciting thing anyone had ever said to me. Here I was, back at Family, ready for my first-ever night as a gigging drag queen.

As soon as I was spotted, I got my invite backstage from a little twink, and I felt like an absolute VIP.

Looking at it, you definitely wouldn't think the drag room was anything special. It was a dank, small space with exposed walls that had shabby old posters representing the history of the queens that had performed there. The room also had a low ceiling, which could barely accommodate the towering drag queens who populated the space, not to mention the twinks who served them.

The room was filled with broken furniture that seemed as if it could fall apart at any moment. Half-drunk glasses, which could have been there for any amount of time, were scattered around. It looked like an irresponsible teenager had taken up residency there, and it was even filthier than my flat.

While it might not have looked appealing, I still felt like I was walking into a penthouse suite. I felt so special to be invited in there, even though the place looked like a complete fucking hole. The condition of the room itself didn't matter. The fact that very few people were invited into the drag room made me feel like I was pretty much in the illuminati.

Despite the fact that the room frequently saw many queens getting ready for shows at once, there were only two mirror stations, each surrounded by lightbulbs, many of which had not been replaced in years. The one on the right-hand side had more functioning lights, which was why that was where Peena Colada liked to get ready. It was her station, and if anyone else dared get ready there without asking, they might not have too many more gigs in their future.

Even though the lightbulbs barely worked and the chair she sat on as she painted her face was broken, Peena Colada still acted as if she was getting ready in a lavish Hollywood trailer. She was Madam Muck, bossing around the gaggle of young gays who surrounded her. I'd never seen anything like it before. These little assistants seemed like they were just there to laugh at her jokes, compliment her looks and run to get whatever she needed at any moment. In the years to come, I'd see them change and rotate, and I was never quite sure what they got out of it. One thing I can say with confidence: it definitely wasn't money.

When I walked in, there were about eight of us in the room: four queens preparing for the show and four of Peena Colada's little minions.

She turned around, looked me up and down, and said, 'Is this your performance costume?'

I didn't understand the question. I had no idea what a 'performance' even meant. I knew drag queens were meant to show up dressed in woman's clothing, but I had no idea what the actual performing component of the evening involved.

I did look lovely, though. Of all the drag looks I'd put together in this early phase, this was surely my most beautiful. I'd taken that night seriously. I'd booked a room at the nearby Grand Millennium Hotel so I could get ready then stroll up to Karangahape Road for the gig. Tabitha had stayed with me to help, but for the first time I'd done my own make-up. I'd even shaved my eyebrows for it so I could draw the new ones on just right.

Peena Colada was the only queen I knew, so I definitely took inspiration from her. I'd painted on big, dramatic, clown-like brows, which made me look a bit surprised, and huge lips and bright colours.

I was so committed to getting it right, I'd bought a size 5XL cream-and-gold corset, which I'd had to pull apart and add fabric to as it didn't fit me. I'd bought a full-on massive bolt of cheap netting fabric and made an enormous skirt. I'd bunched the fabric into a voluminous shape, which in my mind was gorgeous, but in reality made me look ten times bigger than I really was.

I had purchased metre upon metre of fabric for the skirt, thinking, 'OK, well, I want it to be poofy, so, like, I'll just gather it.'

To gather it, I'd basically just sewed the fabric over so there was a channel for the elastic to go through. Then I'd bunched it up on the elastic, which meant my waist was an enormous bulky mass of fabric. But I felt fucking fabulous at the time.

I'd even found some actual cross-dresser shoes with an actual high heel. Unfortunately, I hadn't realised they were in men's shoe sizes, and I'd bought size 11 men's, which are size 14 women's. They were way too big for me, so I was teetering around in them, my feet forward in the heels, as if I was a small boy dressed in his mother's clothing. I had the height I'd lacked during my first time in drag, but I certainly lacked the ability to move with grace.

The centrepiece of the outfit was a pillbox hat I'd made. I'd been to a craft store and bought these little rose details to add to it and they were fucking expensive. I probably spent a hundred and something dollars, which was a ridiculous amount of money for me at the time. I'd spiked my bleached mohawk through the hat, adding a little bit of edge.

I carried a lovely parasol with me – think Mary Poppins going out for a picnic. Those lacy little umbrellas can't really protect you from the sun or the rain. It was as if I'd picked only the daintiest and most ladylike things to counteract my natural body type and spiky hair. I'd gone out of my way to make everything as 'pretty' as possible. I was almost like one of those characters from *Little Britain*, wearing what I thought was ladylike and saying, 'I'm a lady and I do lady things!'

'Yeah, uh, I guess this is my performance outfit.'

'Great, and have you brought a song to perform?'

'Uhhhhh …'

'Deedee, show her the list.'

Deedee Vine, one of the other queens there to perform that night, showed me the list of tracks that were already there and ready to go. At this point, the DJs at Family were still playing everything off CDs, so it wasn't an exhaustive list.

For someone who had grown up listening to goth and rock music, the options were quite limited. I didn't see any songs I knew the words to … except one: 'Teeth', by Lady Gaga. It's quite a rough and dark song, which really didn't match the hungover Mary Poppins look I had assembled.

I had no idea what I was meant to do once the track came on, so I watched the other performances to get a concept for what my performance would be. Unfortunately, I was third in the line-up so I didn't have too much time to think about it.

I barely had the chance to introduce myself to the other people in the drag room. Even Daphne Bush, who I would later become great friends with, seemed terrifying to me that night. As I was all alone, waiting to go on, I was sorely tempted to run straight out of the venue and back to my hotel room. If there had been some kind of back door I could have sneaked out of without anyone noticing, I probably would have done a runner.

I heard my track start and, even though I was ready to shit myself, I stepped out onto the stage. As the music played, something in me stirred and I just went for it. I used the parasol as a prop, whipping it around the stage while dressed like a morbidly obese, dainty lady in lace. It made no sense, but I was being fierce. I was being ferocious. I performed the vibes of the song, even if I didn't quite look the part. It was definitely not a performance the crowd would forget any time soon.

The feeling of performing, the energy of the crowd, the excitement of having all the eyes in Family Bar on me ... it was like nothing I'd ever felt before. I came off the stage with such a rush. I was sweaty, glowing, with a smile I couldn't wipe from my face – and not just because of how big I'd drawn my lips.

'Here's your drink ticket,' said Peena Colada. She was smiling at me. I'd done a good job.

'What'd you think? Do you have any advice?' I asked.

'Go get your drink, hun.'

I learnt pretty quickly that being given your drink ticket was a nice way of Peena Colada telling you it was time to get the hell out of the drag room.

I went out, partied and took compliments from strangers all over the bar. I used my drink ticket and had more drinks bought for me. I danced with Deedee Vine and Daphne Bush and felt like I was one of the girls. Everyone was obsessed with the pillbox hat I'd made, asking me how I'd done it. I regaled them with my adventures with hot glue. For the first time in my life, I felt like I really knew what my thing was.

Just as Tabitha and I were stumbling to the exit, Peena Colada tapped me on the shoulder.

'You were a bit of a mess out there, sweetheart, but I think you've got something. You should come back for this.'

She handed me a flyer with the words 'Princess to Queen: The Competition to find Family Bar's Next Drag Legend' emblazoned on it. I'd found my thing, and now it was time to prove how good I was at it.

When we got back to the hotel, I realised my pillbox hat – the thing I'd spent the whole night bragging about and taking compliments on – was missing. I asked after it every time I went back to the bar for the next few months, but I never saw it again. I have my own theories about where it went.

CHAPTER 6

Getting hooked

THE STORY OF HOW I got the name Kita Mean is not nearly as salacious as you might think. Although it does involve a very special pussy.

I'd never enjoyed going clubbing. It was a place where I, Nick, felt uncomfortable. Surrounded by people who looked like they fitted in at a nightclub, I always felt like I stood out in all the wrong ways. I felt bigger than ever in the cramped, dark spaces, like I was constantly in people's way and like everyone was staring at my awkward attempts at dancing.

When I was in drag at bars, though, I felt like I stood out in all the *right* ways. It gave me the confidence to talk to strangers – I didn't even have to go up and start talking to them, they would approach me. When I had a wig, heels and my very early excuse for make-up on, I felt unstoppable, like the person I'd always wanted to be.

But there was one problem: I didn't know the name of the person I had become. To be honest, I had barely even thought about it. Like many aspects of drag, I hadn't realised the importance of a name or how soon people would want to know what my name was.

One Tuesday night, I headed to Family Bar because I felt like a mid-week dose of attention. I'd assembled a brand-new look with a black, curly wig that definitely did not suit me no matter how hard I tried to style it, and I sat out the front enjoying the stares of the people around me. When people asked who I was, I just said 'Nick', even though that name definitely did not live up to the aesthetic I was presenting.

I wasn't the only drag queen sucking up attention that Tuesday, though. Vudaur Cologne was there with the same idea, looking absolutely gorgeous and put-together in a way I could only dream of. She kept looking over at me, curious about this baby queen she'd never seen before – a baby queen who looked an absolute mess but was clearly feeling herself.

She came up, we got talking and she asked the all-important question: 'So what's your name, queen?'

I panicked. I hadn't even thought about it.

The last time I'd had to think about naming something, I'd made my decision almost right away. My Avondale flat wasn't just filled with rowdy flatmates, it was also home to several feline inhabitants. Karl had a cat which he, very creatively, named Kat. It was spelt with a 'K' as his name was often mistakenly spelt with a 'C', and I guess it meant that he and his kat had something to connect over.

Lisa had a cat too, a black one she named Koki. She is from South Africa and a koki is what they called marker pens there.

I had become obsessed with a film called *Party Monster*, an independent film made by a (then) little-known production studio called World of Wonder. The film is based on the book *Disco Bloodbath* by James St James about his friend, the 'king of the club kids' Michael Alig, who is played in the movie by Macaulay Culkin. It's a wild ride through the intense queer party scene of the 1990s. At one point, the characters break into a vet clinic to steal some ketamine.

Having just adopted a new cat from the SPCA, I thought naming her after a veterinary drug might be appropriate – plus as there was already a 'K' theme running through the names of the flat's cats, I didn't want to upset the balance. But to slightly take the edge off calling her 'ketamine', I thought I should turn it into a cute full name, so she became Kita Mean.

When Vudaur asked what my name was that night, for some reason, without even thinking, I said 'Kita Mean'.

Right away, Vudaur liked the name, and I never considered changing it. Sometimes you need to trust your sudden impulses.

Of course, two queens can't have the same name in one house, so my beautiful animal companion is now known as

Kata-meow. She's fourteen and getting on a bit, so moving around a bit slower, but still every bit as fabulous. Aren't we all?

Years later, on breakfast television, well-known Kiwi broadcaster Paul Henry asked me where I got my name from, and I was very proud to respond: 'I'm named after my pussy.'

* * *

I'd figured out what drag was and I'd come up with a name. Next, I plunged headfirst into the ultra-competitive 'Princess to Queen' competition.

Each Wednesday night for quite a few weeks, Peena Colada hosted a night of amateur queens competing to become Family Bar's new drag superstar. How it was *supposed* to work was, each week, a few queens would compete, and based on the crowd's reaction, one queen would be crowned the winner for that week, though she would not win a prize. After a few weeks of competing, the winners would then face off in a grand finale before a panel of judges. In reality, though, it was not quite so organised. Queens (including myself) would often compete multiple weeks in a row, and to make up the numbers in the finale, there were a few non-winners included in the competition.

I realise now why Peena had likely put on these shows: it was a huge night of entertainment for the audience, but she didn't have to pay any of the acts. I turned up every Wednesday to do my show and I didn't get paid a cent. In fact, I was haemorrhaging money as, each week, I constructed new looks to go with my high-concept ideas.

At the time, I was about a year into studying for a degree in psychology – not that anyone would have known that. All I ever talked about, all I was really focused on, was drag. I treated my studies like a hobby I was vaguely interested in, and I treated drag as though it was my full-time career. But it wasn't my full-time career – I just did a five-minute, unpaid drag performance once a week on a Wednesday. The performances made an impression, though.

Each week, I offered a brand-new show with a completely different look. I lip-synced to 'Halo' by Beyoncé while wearing a giant cardboard spiky mohawk, and a black gown covered in pieces of a mirror-ball that I'd cracked open and glued everywhere. I reused my parasol outfit but added a pink mullet wig to perform to a song by Semi Precious Weapons, just a few weeks after they opened for Lady Gaga. I put everything I had into it.

Every week I was a spectacle, and the crowds loved it. There was an element of excitement and mystery around me. No one had any idea who I was, whereas many of the queens I was competing against were well known on the gay scene before they'd even put on a wig for the first time. People would be like, 'Oh yup, there's James with a wig on!'

For me it was different. I wasn't on the scene, they'd never met me before and, with the size of me, they definitely would have remembered me. No one had any idea what I looked like out of drag, so I was like this enormous drag meteor that had flown in seemingly from nowhere. Ken Ring couldn't have predicted my arrival on the scene, even if he'd read it in my cat's paws!

While most of the other acts were obsessed with being beautiful women, I was doing something that could not have been further away from that. I was freakish, clownish and full of unexpected fun.

I also made my own tracks. Everything was on CD at this point, so most of the queens would just hand over an album and say, 'I think it's track nine … or maybe it's six …'

Not me. I'd spent years playing round with beats on my computer, so I knew how to slice up audio, make my own tracks and burn them onto CDs. Every time, I'd hand my disc over to Peena Colada and say, 'Track one, thanks!'

This made Peena's life easier, and it made me look like a professional woman. 'Track one, thanks!' became my catchphrase, a mark that I knew what I was doing and I hadn't come to play.

There was some fierce competition, though. Truly Scrumptious pulled out gorgeous, funny, campy, classic drag. Gummy Sue was an outrageous act – she was a twenty-something with no teeth who refused to put in falsies. Once, years later, I saw her perform an absolutely insane orange-food-themed act at the short-lived Legend bar, where she crushed those classic cheese-flavoured corn snacks Twisties and Cheezels on her body and sprayed Fanta over the crowd. The twinks whose clothes got sticky hated it, but I loved it.

Despite all the competition, it was pretty clear that one name was all the buzz, and it was mine. The audiences, the bar staff, the queens … everyone was talking about me and anticipating what I would do next. They took note of my clown-like style, my zany performances and my huge energy and started talking about how I was the next Peena Colada.

I wasn't like many of my peers, but I did have some strong similarities to the queen in charge of it all. To be named the next Peena Colada, to be compared to the person who basically ran the Auckland drag scene, was a huge honour for me.

By the time the finale came around, I'd whipped up a massive amount of fans. To be honest, a big part of that was the fact that I'd told every single person in my life how important this was and that I needed them to be there. I reached out to my goth friends, my rock friends, anyone I'd ever worked with or lived with or passed by in the street, and I told them, 'I need you to come and support me. I've never wanted anything more in my life. I want this so badly. If I could ask you just one thing, I would ask that you come to Family Bar to support me in this competition.'

What surprised me was the number of friends I brought with me was matched by the number of people who had come every week and watched my journey along the way.

'Track one, thanks!' I said as I handed the disc over, then I went out and performed to one of my all-time favourite songs, 'Heavy Cross' by Gossip.

I absolutely murdered it on the stage that night. I left nothing behind, gave everything in my performance, feeling every lyric and increasing my intensity with the song's.

By the end, the whole club was chanting 'KITA! KITA! KITA!' I've been told you could hear the chants all the way up K' Road. I put on a show for the ages – and the copy of the CD that I brought along that night is still on a wall at Family, an artefact of the history of the place.

So, I won, obviously. I was over the moon. Yes, there were prizes: a 'grand cash prize', a $100 Costume Magic voucher and a $100 Geoff's Emporium voucher. But what I was really excited about was being recognised for my potential, being seen as the queen I knew I was ready to become.

As the afterparty raged, I saw the judges on their way out. Every week, Peena Colada promised us that some real New Zealand celebrities like Suzanne Paul, who'd become famous for her infomercials selling make-up, would be there, and while that never eventuated, there was a pretty elite team of queer professionals from the New Zealand AIDS Foundation and a few media outlets. One of them was a good friend of my brother, a businesswoman who worked for *Express* magazine.

As she left, I thanked her for the win, and was surprised by her reply: 'You deserved it. We really had to fight for you up there.'

Huh? People were chanting my name; you could hear it down the street … but I almost hadn't taken it out. I couldn't make sense of it.

* * *

It was a good thing I hadn't really cared about the prizes because I didn't get all of them. I did get *some* prizes, just not in the way I expected.

When I heard I was getting a $100 Geoff's Emporium voucher, I was stoked. Geoff's Emporium is a wet dream to a crafty artist like Kita: a giant shop filled with everything you need to build, make and sew your creations. Fabric, paints, party goods, a charming middle-aged woman who's always up for a chat while you shop … the store had it all. I expected a gift voucher I could take to the store and shop to my heart's content, but that's not quite what I got.

Instead, I had to make an appointment to meet Peena Colada and her friend Miss Kay at the store. They would then follow me around while I chose what I wanted – some wigs, some fabric, everything I could get within the budget – then

Peena paid for it. It was an awkward experience for me, while, for them, it was their first time seeing me out of drag.

The first thing Miss Kay said to me was, 'Jesus, you're a big boy, aren't you?'

So, it was not exactly the friendliest shopping day. I can understand why she was surprised, though – when you see someone in drag it can be pretty hard to know just how much fabric and padding there is, and exactly what's underneath. In the cold light of day that morning on Dominion Road, the real me was truly on show.

After the pair of them had stalked me around the shop and most likely judged the shit out of the items I was choosing, I was a bit nervous to ask about the other prizes I had won.

A few more days went by, and there was no word on the other things I was supposed to receive. I hounded Peena every few days about the other prizes. It wasn't even really about feeling like I deserved them, I just wanted some kind of return for the time and money I had put into Princess to Queen every single week.

The Costume Magic voucher never eventuated, which was fine because it probably would have involved another extremely awkward trip to the shops with Peena and Kay.

The cash prize did eventually come my way, though also not in the way I had expected. I saw Peena Colada at the bar one night, well over a month after the competition was over, and I asked once again when I could expect to get the prize.

'Today's your lucky day,' she said with a sly smile. She handed me her bank card, told me her pin number and told me to get $100 cash out at the ATM.

I was confused, but I did it. I'm a trustworthy person so I didn't even take the chance to look at her bank balance, even though I now wish I had. I returned to the bar, and handed her the card and the cash. She took them, then handed the cash straight back to me.

'Here's your prize, darling.'

'Uh … thanks …'

I was so confused. I was sure the poster had advertised a 'grand cash prize'. I started to second-guess myself — maybe I'd got it wrong? But as I left the bar that night, I saw a poster for the competition still hanging up on the wall. Clear as day, it said: 'GRAND CASH PRIZE'. How could a grand cash prize be $100?

I didn't want to have a confrontation, but I needed that cash. After all, I had spent a lot on the competition already, I had brought it every time, and I had also brought plenty of people to the bar. If you actually tabulated the hours I had put in, even $1000 would have been a pretty measly payment. So I sent an email through to Wayne, who owned the bar. In it I wrote:

Hi my name is Kita.

I just did Princess to Queen. I was there every week and won the finale. The prize that was actually given to me was $100 cash and, because it was advertised as a grand cash prize, I just wanted to confirm if this is what I was supposed to be getting? Was that the prize?

Best wishes,

Kita Mean

I never got a reply, which is in many ways the most terrifying reply you can receive. I'd almost forgotten about the email until one night I arrived at Family Bar and got a bit of a shock.

'Peena Colada would like to see you in the drag room.'

This was nowhere near as exciting as it had been the first time I'd heard those words. I walked backstage to see Peena looking like Cersei Lannister in *Game of Thrones*, surrounded by a royal family of evil drag queens, drag hags and twink servants. I sat down in front of her. It was deathly quiet for a moment, then she launched into her tirade.

'Who the FUCK do you think you are, emailing Family Bar, going over my head? The flagrant disregard for everything I've given you ... I made you ...' It went on and on.

I tried to apologise: 'I just thought that the prize was more than that, so I wanted to check what had happened.'

By now, I was sobbing, in front of a room full of people I was desperate to impress.

'Well, you were wrong. Never go behind my back like this again!'

When she was finished, I went downstairs. I had tears running down my face and no more cash in my wallet.

All I had to show from winning what was, at the time, the biggest drag competition in the country was $100, a few metres of fabric and a couple of wigs from Geoff's. I did get a crown on the night I won, but it went missing almost immediately. I know it might sound like I just lose things, but I suspect some shady-boots numbers were getting pulled there.

One night when Peena wasn't at Family, I asked Grady, who worked behind the bar, if I could take an A4 poster for the competition that was hanging up in the corner of the drag room, so I had something to remember it by.

'Of course, I don't see why not! You were the winner, after all,' he said. It was nice to be reminded of that.

I didn't think anyone would even notice that the poster was gone, but I should have known better. Nothing goes unnoticed at Family Bar. The next time I was back there, across the wall where the poster had hung, scrawled in black marker pen was:

POSTER STOLEN, WHO???

I guess someone must have solved the mystery, because just a few weeks later it read:

POSTER STOLEN, WHO???

KITA MEAN! DOG!!!

I have no idea whether or not it was Peena who wrote those messages – it could just as easily have been one of her many minions – but someone at Family Bar clearly hated me.

CHAPTER 7

Working girl

FORTUNATELY FOR ME, I was talented and – probably more importantly – available and keen, so Peena Colada continued to book me. Every time an event came up for which she needed a bunch of queens who she knew could perform well, I'd get the call.

'Kiiiiiiiiita, something's come up and I thought of *you* straight away, gorgeous. Your call time is two hours before the show starts, bring two outfits and do two numbers and I will *not* take no for an answer. Anyway, see you there, doll! Love ya!'

It was so strange. The person who had brought me into a private room in front of my peers to scold me for asking for money I believed I'd won was now acting as though she was my best friend.

Slowly, I came to realise there was a common thread to the times she got in touch. It would normally be for events like fundraisers, the bar's birthday celebrations – the type of events that needed big line-ups and, more noticeably, did not pay. For a long time, I didn't mind this. I loved drag and I wanted to do it as much as possible. I hadn't even really considered that it could be a full-time job at this point, so any time I got the call I couldn't have been more excited to doll myself up for a show. Also, the more shows I did, the more I realised I had serious talent for it. I watched all the other queens, then I watched the way the crowd responded to me. The only other queen who could get the crowd as amped up as I could was Peena Colada herself.

I could feel my star rising, but there was a big glass of fruit drink in my way. Peena Colada seemed to control the drag hierarchy. I wanted to stay on her good side because, from where I was sitting, it seemed that if I pissed her off again, my drag career would be over. She was the great gatekeeper, and I didn't want to be shut outside of the gate to this new world that made me feel like I had fully become myself.

I wanted more gigs. I wanted to perform at more places than just Family, and I wanted to get my drag seen by more people. I knew there were some queens out there who would never be booked on the same line-ups as me because they were dead to Peena Colada.

Tess Tickle was someone I had heard a lot about but had never met. She was a legend of the scene, a queen who really knew how to put on a show, how to run a business and how to earn the respect of her peers. Peena Colada bad-mouthed Tess every chance she got, but every time she did, it became more and more clear it was because she felt threatened. I decided that if Tess was a threat to Peena Colada, she must be talented. I had to meet her.

I met one of Tess's best friends and another legend of the drag scene, Buckwheat, at a new gay bar called Naval & Family. She invited me along to DNA, which was another of Auckland's new gay bars. (Mentioning all these places makes me nostalgic for a time when Auckland had more than just three nightclubs for queers!)

DNA had only just opened and Tess had taken up residency as a host. There weren't many queens qualified to host, so Tess getting this job had pissed off some other queens at that level. I decided that if Buckwheat could introduce me to Tess, at least it wouldn't be awkward. I was wrong. It was extremely awkward.

I arrived in drag, the only way I felt confident enough to go to a bar. I'd entered the queer party scene as Kita Mean, and it would be years before I would get enough confidence to go out as Nick. Even on a night like this, when I was just going out for a drink and to (possibly) meet someone for the first time, I'd put on a full drag look. It was my superhero uniform. It gave me the courage to meet new people and let go of myself a little, but even it wasn't helping me on this night.

Buckwheat greeted me at the front of the bar. 'Kita, sweetie! You actually came!'

She gave me a huge hug and walked me backstage. There, Tess was getting ready to do what we call a production show – a fully choreographed show with a cast of at least three or four queens, as opposed to a line-up show of queens performing their own spots. It's not really a full production – but for us hard-hustling queens, it feels like one.

It was a tiny little backroom behind the bar, with barely enough room to fit one drag queen, let alone three, but it still felt like the height of professionalism to me. (DNA is now a Spanish restaurant called Carmen Jones, so I can only imagine this 'dressing room' is where they now store their mops and brooms.)

All of Tess's wigs were lined up together, and this was the first time I had ever seen anything like it. I imagined being able to choose between all of these instead of just combing out the only Two Dollar Shop one I could afford!

And there was Tess. She looked gorgeous and more than ready to do her show, but ever the perfectionist, she was examining every detail of her make-up and outfit to make sure she looked just right. She was really concentrating, and here I was interrupting.

I stood awkwardly in the corner, feeling like a crazy fan who had broken into a celebrity's house. It didn't feel like she was ready to meet some random.

'Tess,' Buckwheat interrupted after a moment of intense silence, as Tess delicately placed a set of lashes on her eye. 'This is that queen Kita, you know, the one everyone's been talking about.'

Tess turned, looked me up and down, smiled in a way that felt like it was mainly to be polite and said, 'Hi, darling,' before returning to her mirror.

'I'll leave you to it, girl,' said Buckwheat, rushing out of the room as quickly as she had rushed us in.

I watched as Tess refined the tiniest details of her beautiful beat. From where I was standing, it didn't look like there was anything to improve on, and maybe there wasn't, maybe she was just pretending to focus so she wouldn't have to talk to me.

I was standing there for probably only a few minutes, but it felt like the longest few minutes of my entire life. Eventually, I had to break the silence. I'd been scanning through my head for every possible conversation starter I could think of. Ultimately, all I could muster was: 'I'm just going to go get a drink. I'm pretty thirsty.'

'All right, girl. See you out there,' Tess said. It was pretty clear she was not going to miss my presence.

I felt like it could not have gone worse. But sometimes amazing things can have terrible beginnings. I didn't know it then, but I had just met my drag mother.

* * *

I don't know if I tainted the place by being such an awkward mess, but DNA closed its doors pretty soon after. Sadly, the size of Auckland and the fickleness of its gay scene means that our queer spaces often end up like frozen yoghurt shops – they open with a hiss and a roar but then, before anyone even realises it, they are gone.

From the ashes of DNA, a new venue called Switch Bar rose up like a phoenix. It didn't last forever, but it had a big impact on the scene. It was also the setting for one of my most important nights in drag. (The letters on the outside of Switch Bar were re-ordered a few years later when an alcohol-free bar called Twist opened and then closed not long after.)

Every Thursday, Tess hosted a competition at Switch Bar where two queens would compete in a battle, and only one would win. Much like the Princess to Queen competition, it was a great way for the bar to offer entertainment without having to fork out money to pay the performers, but there was a distinctly different vibe. Immediately, it felt more supportive and, as performers and competitors, we were taken care of.

I performed in two of the heats, winning one of them and getting robbed in the other (I assume, I don't remember!). Even so, I made it through to the finals of the competition. For the finale, I wanted to do something different from anything anyone had seen me do before – and, as it turned out, something no one would ever see me do again. I decided to sing a cappella. It's one of the riskiest things a performer can do, and, from experience, I'm happy to tell you that the risk did not pay off.

My performance was of the iconic song 'Poor Unfortunate Souls', which is performed by Ursula in Disney's *The Little Mermaid*. From when I was a kid, I'd always connected with Ursula. As little gay Nick watching the cartoon over and over again on VHS, there was something that instantly drew me to her. Years later, this suddenly made sense when I found out the character was designed to look like the ultimate drag legend Divine.

I loved the song and I knew I could carry a tune, so I organised what I needed for the show that – in my mind – was going to bring the house down. I had a huge cardboard cauldron that I spent days working on, a fabulous Ursula outfit with giant tentacles made of silver vinyl fabric, and I even organised an expensive headset microphone to pick up what I was sure was going to be my exceptional vocals.

I was up near the end of the line-up, among all these queens who had won their heats. They all did fabulous numbers to high-energy songs. As I sat backstage, I was so sure that what I was about to do would give everybody goosebumps. No music, just my voice? It would surely be the moment everyone talked about.

I was announced, and there was silence. That's what I wanted, obviously, but it certainly didn't feel like a comfortable silence. After so many exhilarating lip-sync numbers, the mood shift stood out for all the wrong reasons. It was clear the vibe in the room was not what I had hoped for.

I started singing, but I could barely hear myself. I'd sound-checked while the venue was almost completely empty, but now that it was full of people the acoustics were wildly different. Keeping up with my own rhythm and staying in one key was all but impossible. I soldiered through the song, with no response from the audience apart from a few coughs. I tried to channel my inner Ursula, to be expressive, big and camp, but on the inside I felt the opposite: embarrassed, small and silly.

After a smattering of clapping, I left the stage knowing I'd absolutely fucked up. I so admired Tess, so to do this in front of her shattered me.

Just in case it isn't already abundantly clear, I didn't win the crown. In fact, while there weren't any official rankings, I'd wager that I'd been right at the bottom of the list. To make things worse, I had to wait around for hours before I could leave. I didn't want the crowd, who had watched me perform, to see me. I was too humiliated to walk past them carrying my folded-down cauldron of shame.

As the bar was winding down for the night, I finally started to pack down my stuff. I think it was pretty clear from the way I was packing up my things that I was in a bit of an emotional state. Tess could see that, and she wasn't going to let me suffer on my own.

'Babe, don't worry,' she said, not even bothering to lie to me that my performance had been good. 'Look, you had a strong vision and you believed in your vision, and that says a lot about your commitment to your craft and your conviction in your performances.'

I started crying immediately. 'I'm just so embarrassed that I did that in front of so many people. It was a complete bomb. Why did I ever think that was going to work?'

She smiled at me. 'Look, babe, I should have said something at rehearsal. As soon as I saw you setting up your microphone, I knew what was going to happen. I've just spent the whole night wishing I'd come up and said to you right then, "Let's get you a backing track". It would have made your life so much easier. I just didn't want to mess with what you had planned and I knew you must've put so much into it but … you know what … I'm an older, experienced girl and I just should have given you some advice. I've been beating myself up over it all night.'

In the space of just a few minutes, she had given me more empathy and mentorship than I'd ever received from any other queen. To have her reach out like that, at a time when I was at my lowest, touched me right in the ticker – and I think I touched her heart as well.

She saw how passionate I was, how much I loved what I did and how lofty my goals for myself were. Even though she'd just seen me do my worst performance ever, this was the start of a long and bountiful friendship.

* * *

'And afterwards I'll need you to email through your invoice, but you have to pay your own tax.'

'I'm sorry, what?'

Pretty soon after having watched me completely confuse an audience with my a cappella disaster, it became clear to me that Tess Tickle had seen something in me that she thought was worth paying for. I was being offered my first paid gigs performing at Switch Bar on Friday nights, and she wasn't just giving me work, she was mentoring me into becoming a fully professional queen.

'You show up one hour before curtain, arrive ready in your first look, but bring an outfit change for the second show. You don't drink on the job and you email your invoice the next morning if you want to be paid on time. And most importantly, babe, always bring a good show. I'm paying you, babe, so none of that sad *Little Mermaid* shit.'

I didn't instantly make bank. In fact, it would be a long time before I made anywhere near the amount of money I needed to pay myself back for the drag I'd been buying. I still had to cut financial corners all the time. I had to store my drag in the garage at my flat, because I only had a small room. Heaps of my costumes went mouldy as a result, but I just had to keep wearing them.

I tried to get whatever costume pieces I could for free. My

bras, for instance, came from my sister Sophie. She was bigger like me, so she had these massive boulder-holder bras that were perfect for me. When her bras started getting a bit busted, she would give them to me. I didn't need the underwires so I would pull them out, and I'd wear those bras until they were completely worn through.

Every few months, Sophie would text me: 'Hey big bro, do you need more bras?'

I'd reply, 'Keep 'em coming!'

She was like my Recycle Boutique, but just for bras – and those things are expensive! It would be a long time before I started buying my own, so if you saw me in the first eight years of my drag career, I was probably wearing my little sister's bra!

My sister's bras were not the only family item that was pulled into my drag. My mother also contributed some costume items, although she was not aware of it. Good ol' Bridget let me sleep on her couch for a month or so when I was in between flats, and it gave me a great opportunity to forage through all of her things. While she was at work, I would look through the drawers and cupboards for things that I could glitter up and wear onstage.

My mother has always had these fancy possessions that she'd describe in her BBC voice. She does love her posh things. She has dozens of pairs of shoes that are just displayed on shelves, and are not for wearing. There are fancy ornaments all around her house.

One thing she particularly loved was a fancy feather duster. It was made of the most beautiful rooster feathers and it had a gorgeous wooden handle. Even though it was designed to be used around the house, it was so nice that Mum never used it for cleaning. It was a display piece that was even too fancy to have on display all the time, so it mostly stayed safely tucked away in a cupboard.

At the time, feathers were hard to come by. This was before the days of AliExpress, so being able to source random draggy items was not as simple as a few clicks. Instead, we had to hunt things down from op-shops, friends and family.

I stared at the feather duster and, immediately, it was giving me drag fabulousness. It made me think of the feather duster in Disney's *Beauty and the Beast*, and I knew I could use it for something. I had a foam headdress that was looking a bit worse for wear, but I didn't like to throw anything out. I plucked the feathers off the duster, dyed them and created a massive plume to go on the top of that headpiece. It was so fucking cool.

It looked so good I didn't even attempt to hide it from my mum.

'Hey, check out what I made!'

'Oh, my goodness, honey, that's glorious. You're so talented. That is beautiful.'

She had no idea.

A couple of weeks after I moved out of her house, she called me. 'Hey sweetie, have you seen my duster? I've got this really expensive duster that I had put away. It's beautiful, that's why I kept it hidden. You'd know it if you saw it. It was gorgeous. Do you know where it might be?'

'Hmm … no idea, sorry, Mum!'

'Are you sure? Because I remember you showed me that fabulous headdress a few weeks ago, and those looked like the same type of feathers that were on the duster.'

'No way, Mum. I got those feathers from a shop called … umm … Hey Girl! They do all the best drag stuff.'

For years, she would bring it up, hoping I would crack. I've got a message for you, Mum: Fine, I'll pay you back!

The more we worked together, the more Tess took opportunities to help me level up my drag and become a better queen.

Pretty soon, Limelight Cabaret, who ran travelling drag and cabaret shows across Tāmaki Makaurau, needed another queen for their line-up. (You'll hear a bit more about Limelight later.)

Clearly impressed with what I was delivering, Tess told me, 'I believe in you. You've proven that you're responsible. You've proven that you're reliable. You've proven that you're really putting energy into how you present yourself.'

Hearing those words from her meant so much. To have my work ethic and my passion noticed meant more to me than anything. It's hard to say when we made it official, but it was pretty clear to me that Tess had become my new drag mother.

She continued to give me more and more opportunities and, each time, she saw me rise to the occasion. If it weren't for her guidance, I would not be half the queen I am today … and, no, that is *not* a weight-loss joke.

Despite all she'd done for me, I was still pretty shocked when she asked me to take a much bigger leap.

Just as things were picking up for Tess at Limelight, Switch Bar needed a new host. Tess asked me if I would take on this massive role. At the time, there were only really three queens on the scene who hosted at clubs: Tess, Buckwheat and Peena Colada. For me to be asked, when I was still essentially a baby queen, was a huge honour.

Essentially, becoming a host means the owner of the club trusts you to run a full night of entertainment. You curate the show, organise the performers, and act as the event organiser ahead of the show. If anyone doesn't show up or isn't up to par, it's on your shoulders. Then, on the night, you also MC the show itself. It's a demanding, rigorous role that not everyone can do – and I loved it!

I already knew that doing drag was my passion, but when I started hosting I truly fell head over heels for drag all over again. As a hostess, I got to really let rip, and once I started talking into that microphone, I was so in my element you'd have had to rip it out of my cold, dead, drag hands to stop me.

Between each act, I roamed around the room, chatting to the crowd and brewing up huge laughs. I'd always had an outrageous sense of humour, but this finally let me show just how quick I was. The way I could turn anything into a filthy pun in seconds made me a machine.

There was something about announcing the acts that I got a real kick out of. When we were growing up, my older brother Matt always watched wrestling. I'd got into it too, partly because I wanted to fit in with my big bro, but also because I loved the outrageousness and the spectacle of it. I particularly adored the way the announcers would introduce each wrestler, with full gusto: 'Let's get rrready to rrrrrrumble!'

Now I got to do that, but with drag queens instead of wrestlers, and, really, what are wrestlers but drag queens for straight men? Wrestling is pure proof that straight men are into the same flamboyant, outrageously camp shit that we are – they just need to have it in a slightly more masculine form, so they can live in their fantasy. Sorry to ruin it for you, heteros!

It had been two years since I'd started out, met Peena Colada and competed in Princess to Queen. I'd come such a long way, but I was still doing those occasional gigs for Peena when she needed a queen. I'd managed to smooth things over with her, not because I wanted to but out of necessity – she was the one booking the gigs at the biggest gay bar in town.

I booked every gig I could. I loved performing, and our relationship seemed like it was back in a more positive space. That was until one fateful night, when I found out exactly what she had been up to.

* * *

It was Priscilla night at Silo Park. They were screening the classic drag film, *The Adventures of Priscilla, Queen of the Desert*, down by the waterfront. The film was being projected onto one of the massive silos from which the park gets its name, and – to add some extra fabulousness – they'd hired Tess and me to provide entertainment throughout the night.

We were sitting backstage, which was inside the silo the film was being projected onto, when Tess suddenly got a very serious look on her face.

'What's wrong?' I asked.

'Babe, I need to tell you something. But it's not going to be easy to hear. It's about … you-know-who …'

At the time, everything between me and Peena Colada had felt pretty amicable. We worked together, we'd have a drink together after gigs, and we'd say 'hi' if we crossed paths on K' Road. But it turned out she hadn't been speaking so kindly about me when I wasn't around.

Tess unloaded. According to her, ever since the Princess to Queen competition, Peena had been out to get me. Everyone had been saying that I was 'the new Peena Colada' and her 'mini-me', and with good reason. I was a campy queen with loud costumes and a quick wit, and what I served up was basically a fresher version of what Peena did. This clearly hadn't been sitting well with her.

'Look, babe, I was at a big meeting with the New Zealand AIDS Foundation and your name came up.' I could tell Tess felt awkward about whatever she was about to tell me.

'People were mentioning you, you know, "There's this new baby queen, Kita, who we could get to do some work with us ..." and, as soon as your name was mentioned, old Miss Colada just went off. She absolutely ran your name into the ground. She said you and your whole family are alcoholics, that you are the most unreliable person she had ever met in her life and that the foundation should have absolutely nothing to do with you.'

It was like a ton of bricks had slapped me in the face. This person I had opened up to and idolised was ruining my name with the AIDS Foundation, an organisation I was desperate to impress and work with.

She wasn't just a queen I'd looked up to a little; she was the first queen I'd ever met and the first queen I'd ever seen perform. Watching her perform, I'd seen what I wanted to be, and now she'd revealed herself to be the sort of person I never, ever wanted to be.

I'd spent nights after gigs telling her my life story and talking about things I had struggled with. Had she really warped those stories so far from what I had said? And for what? So I wouldn't steal even a tiny bit of her work?

More stories emerged over the following weeks and months after that. The friend of my brother who had been a judge for Princess to Queen told me that even back then, when I was just starting out, the talk of me being similar to Peena Colada filled Peena with spite. That night, when the whole bar had been chanting my name, she reckoned Peena had argued with the other judges, saying she wanted one of the other queens to win.

I was told the other judges had had to go against her completely to get her to award me the crown. I was flabbergasted.

* * *

Even though my drag career was going from strength to strength, I still needed a day job to fund my moonlighting in drag, so I was working full-time in sales for an internet provider, having worked my way up from their IT troubleshooting team (sheer insanity, as I wasn't internet savvy *at all*). Living between those two worlds as Nick and Kita, I was so busy that I started to see my family less and less. I was living life out west when they lived out east, and not by any intention it became that I only saw Mum or Dad for birthdays or Christmas. We all just had our own thing going on.

Meanwhile, my drag family was expanding. Around this time, I was living in Mount Albert with my fabulous, loyal and fierce friend Trinity Ice. In the backyard of our flat there, I met my drag daughter for the first time – and I met her because she just piped up and started chatting to us.

Trinity and I were rushing to get into drag for a gig that night when I heard a little voice from over the hedge.

'Hello?'

It was an adorable human from a provincial town in Hawke's Bay, who now goes by the name Kendra.

Kendra's parents hadn't handled the whole coming out thing very well, so she had packed up her things and moved straight to the big smoke to start living the queer life.

I don't know how she'd got so lucky, or what would have happened if she'd moved in somewhere else, but this little, shy, queer kid ended up living next door to two chatty drag queens who helped introduce her to Auckland.

I could see from the way she looked at our things that she loved drag. I didn't know if she'd tried drag before her big move, but I could tell she was definitely keen to try it now.

Almost every day, she'd come over to our place, and – even though she lived right next door – she ended up sleeping on our couch most of the time. I could tell she loved being at our place and that she never wanted to leave.

She was definitely from a different background to us. Sometimes she almost seemed like a *Mean Girls* character come to life. Her parents must have been pretty well off because the way she talked about them was wild. She would refer to her mum by her first name – Vanessa – and clearly had pretty high expectations of her: 'If Vanessa doesn't get me a new phone for Christmas I'm never talking to her again!'

Even though she came from immense privilege in terms of money, Kendra clearly had not been given the opportunity to explore and express herself as a queer person. I took her under my wing and started teaching her the ways of drag. The first thing I taught her about doing drag was that she needed to get herself a normal job.

She didn't have money coming in from her parents anymore, and she needed to pay her rent. Plus, if she ever wanted to make it in the drag scene, she needed to buy some drag to put on. After all, my hand-me-downs would only get her so far.

What started as a friendship with a neighbour quickly became a relationship of mentoring and nurturing. It felt like my drag journey had barely begun, but there I was, already someone's drag mother.

Felicia Diamond was her drag name, even though I tried my best to get her to change it. Such a glamorous name just didn't suit the queen she actually was. Her drag ended up being pretty camp … she was learning from me after all!

She was a large-and-in-charge crazy bitch, and I told her time and time again that she should be called Felicia Thunderthighs. I so thought that name suited her that I would introduce her as that, and I would play AC/DC's 'Thunderstruck' as she came on stage. It was epic, camp and fun. She hated it.

Hers was an amazing act. She could sing, like, *really* sing. A drag artist who could sing was pretty rare in Tāmaki

Makaurau at the time, and that exciting niche meant I could line her up with some pretty decent private-party gigs.

I was driving a tiny, two-door Toyota Cynos, which was just perfect for when I was fully dressed in drag. Trinity Ice, Felicia and I would travel to gigs in it, and we looked like three enormous clowns when we got out of it, like there was no way we could possibly have fitted in there.

Felicia had an iconic look and energy. This gentle giant was such a big human being that she just could not find shoes that fit her. Her feet were size 16, so she couldn't exactly pick up a pair of heels from the store. As a result, she was usually about four sizes bigger than the shoes she was wearing. To get around this, she ended up cutting the backs of her shoes off and using ropes to tie them to the back of her ankle and up her leg. She could fit maybe three toes, maximum, in the front of each shoe, and the others would stick out the side of the straps. Her actual heels would hang outrageously far back from the heel of the shoe, and it looked hilarious.

I was the one who ordered her the first pair of high heels that actually fitted her. We measured her feet, so we had the specs exactly, and then I got them sent over from the United States. They weren't that flash, but she was over the moon when she got them. Looking back now and knowing that she is a transgender woman, though she wasn't out as trans at that point in time, I can see why that had such a massive impact for her. I'm so happy I got to give her those shoes.

She was doing great and rising up the scene fast … so it wasn't too long before she met Peena Colada. And that is when things got messy.

Peena had recently started performing at Limelight Cabaret, so we had become more involved with each other again. Once she met Felicia, Peena took quite a liking to her. At this point, I had not been super public about how I felt about Peena. However, Felicia was about to make things a bit spicier between us.

I'd been helping Felicia get her CV together and find the right sort of jobs that would work alongside drag, so when she got an interview I was so proud of her, I bought her a present and everything. I guess her privileged Hawke's Bay past resurfaced, though, because when the day of the interview came, she just didn't go.

'I just wasn't feeling it today.'

OK, girl. I hate to break it to you, but we all have to work regardless of whether we are 'feeling it' or not.

Being a mother is obviously about showing love, but it's not about coddling. I was mad at her and I wanted to teach her a lesson. I knew how much she loved drag, and she would often get all dolled up to come with me and Trinity to our Limelight gigs.

I told her flat out, 'This weekend, you can't come to our shows. I don't want to see you in drag. You don't put the work in, so you don't get to come out and have fun.'

Later, I found out Peena Colada went and picked Felicia up and brought her to our gig. I was incensed.

I cornered Peena backstage. 'I am trying to teach this girl the ways of the world. And I would appreciate it if you could let me be a mother to my drag daughter. If she doesn't learn, she will never make it in this industry.'

I guess I must have scared her because she apologised and seemed to go quiet for the rest of the night.

A few days later, though, she was back to full blast. Peena Colada turned up at my house, knocked once on the door, then started screaming.

My flatmate answered the door then came to get me, terrified by what he had just seen.

When I got to the door, Peena started barking in my face. 'Who are you? Do you know who I am? How dare you talk to me like that!'

I reached my limit of her yelling pretty quickly, so I went to slam the door in her face. But she stuck her foot in the way!

'The only reason you don't want Felicia to come to Limelight is because you're jealous of her. She's prettier than you!' she went on.

I looked her dead in her eyes. 'Come on, bitch. I'm not jealous of Felicia. In fact, the entire Auckland drag scene thinks that you're jealous of *me*. So, you can take that comment and get out of my face!'

When I threatened to call the cops, she left with her tail between her legs.

It was such an intense interaction and I don't know where I'd got the courage to say that to her, but I loved it. It rolled out so easily, and, even though I felt scared of what might happen next, I was proud of myself too.

For me, this was the point of no return with Peena Colada. We had both gone too far. She had turned up at my house to roar in my face. I had told her, plain and simple, that I knew she was jealous of me. It was all out in the open.

If I'm truthful, I was scared. I knew how much power she had in the drag community. But I was also prepared. I knew how much power I had inside myself.

* * *

After everything that happened between me and this queen who I'd spent years idolising and who I wanted to prove myself to so much, it's tempting to look back and wish that she'd never been in my life.

But, to be honest with you, I'm grateful for her and what she did. It all served to light a fire under me. Every bad thing that was said set me directly on a course to actively prove her wrong.

I'm unreliable? I make a point of being on time for every gig, of replying to every email, of never letting anyone down.

I'm an alcoholic? I make sure to maintain a high level of extreme professionalism in every job I do.

I know in my heart that all of the bad energy came because she was told time and time again that I was similar to her. Maybe it scared her to have someone else doing what she did.

Unfortunately for her, she was never going to be the only campy queen in Auckland. My act, my looks and my personality have evolved so much since then that those comparisons aren't really accurate anymore anyway.

For me, knowing that I had something similar to someone else in my field didn't make me want to tear them down, it just made me want to be better, to work and work and work until there was no question over who the best campy queen in Auckland was.

As I get older and a new generation of queens starts emerging, I can definitely understand the fears and insecurity my sudden rise to fame might have caused. But I have determined, in myself, to never act in the ways she did.

As an established part of the Aotearoa drag scene, it is my job to lift others up, to provide mentorship and friendship, and to support them with opportunities. I even met a little someone I shared the name Nick with, who I would come to know as Anita Wigl'it, and together we started to do just that.

* * *

Before we move on, I need to talk about what happened to my daughter Felicia Diamond. I often refer to Felicia in the past tense, but that is not because she passed away, so don't worry! She has been through a tumultuous journey, though, and she no longer performs in drag.

Felicia rose fast in the drag scene, but it wasn't happening fast enough for her and – because she never got herself a day job to make ends meet – she ended up working as an escort. I am definitely pro sex work, but I don't think it's for everyone.

Trinity was a sex worker as well, so she helped show Kendra the ropes. I was a little nervous for poor Kendra – she was so young and I just didn't have full confidence in her ability to take care of herself in such a tough industry.

After a few months, she began her transition, which was when she first claimed the name Kendra. Felicia was gone pretty soon after she transitioned, but I, as her mother, am still allowed to call her that.

She ended up making the move to Australia to continue the process of becoming her authentic self. It seemed like a good move – the money is way better there and so are the resources for people who are transitioning. But things were tough, and pretty soon she started taking meth. I heard what was going on, but it was hard to make contact with Kendra and even harder to give her advice.

Relatively quickly, she started going off the rails, having become fully reliant on drugs. She wouldn't respond when I tried to get in touch, so I felt helpless. With a whole ocean separating us, I was no longer in the position to give her the tough love that might have helped.

After months of watching her destructive behaviour from across the ditch, I had to take a step away. I told her, 'Look, I can't control you. I've tried everything I can, but if you are not going to listen to me, that is your prerogative. I care deeply about you, but I'm not your real mother. If you don't want to help yourself, I don't know what more I can do.'

From there, things got worse for her. When I say worse, I mean life-threateningly bad. Her meth addiction took over her life and she even ended up using injectables. It's a path that a lot of our trans sisters and sex workers end up on, because they get pushed out to the fringes by our still extremely conservative systems.

Society constantly makes things harder for our trans whānau, and trans women who work in the sex industry are regarded extremely poorly. Purely as a result of people's own prejudices, these women are treated as lesser humans and their lives seem to have little value to the people calling the shots. It's a true tragedy, and something I hope continues to shift thanks to positive changes in our human rights laws and greater and more varied representation in our media.

Things ended up getting so dangerous and Kendra got in so much trouble that she had to make the call to make some changes. It shouldn't have to be this way, but when people hit rock bottom it sometimes leads them back to the path they should be on and want to be on.

Kendra got out of the bad circles she was in, moved back to Aotearoa and gave up drugs. She's continued as a sex worker, but she no longer puts herself in vulnerable or risky situations. She got together enough money to train for a new job, and she's recently learnt how to do microblading, which she's really good at. She's a queen once again, just in a slightly different field.

I'm so proud of her. It's been a bumpy road, and, even though she doesn't do drag anymore, I still feel a sense of responsibility as her drag mother. Our relationship has truly felt, to some degree, like that of a parent and child. I love her like a parent would. I want to see her succeed. I want to give her everything I can to help her succeed. I was ashamed of her fallen steps and I am proud of her achievements. It truly feels like she's my daughter.

We keep in touch and there's no bad blood between us. I see her whenever we are in the same town, and we banter just like old times. I'm the only person that is still allowed to call her Felicia, and whenever I call her that it truly warms my heart. (She still doesn't like being called Thunderthighs, though. Fair enough, she never did!)

It's been a wild ride, but I'll always be grateful that she piped up over the fence of my and Trinity's flat and asked to hang out.

CHAPTER 8

Business bitch

THE GAY NIGHTLIFE SCENE in Tāmaki Makaurau is a difficult place to make a living. Probably the most well-known place to watch drag in Aotearoa, Caluzzi, actually began its life as a cafe. During the day, it would serve its coffees and muffins, then close before it got dark. Back then, having a Norah Jones CD playing over the speakers was the closest it got to having any sort of drag show.

For whatever reason, the cafe had ended up with quite a few queer people on staff, and some of them loved to drag up at the end of the night before heading out to livelier spots along Karangahape Road. Some of their customers started to notice this, and they would linger over their cakes and sandwiches until the place was closing, eager to get a gander at the waitstaff's transformations.

Eventually, the customers didn't want to just see the looks – they wanted a whole damn show, so Caluzzi put on a drag-and-dinner show in 1996. It was so successful, they put on another. And then another. And then so many more that they closed down the cafe aspect of the venue and it became a full-time drag-and-dinner theatre. Every Aucklander knows it now. Even if they haven't been inside the place, they will have driven past and seen the queens making use of the street outside Caluzzi as they perform through the windows for their paying guests while giving pedestrians and passing motorists a free show at the same time.

After Caluzzi's drag-and-dinner shows had been slaying the game for some time, a woman named Arlana Delamere took her parents, including her well-known politician dad, Tuariki Delamere, to Caluzzi and pitched her idea for a new drag venue to them. She wanted to offer a similar night of entertainment but levelled up. She wanted the space to be more like a theatre, with proper lights, big sound, smoke machines and all that jazz.

With the help of a reasonable-sized investment from her parents, she opened Finale in 2003, about 100 metres further up K' Road. She then proceeded to hire some of Auckland's best queens including Ling Ling, Felisha Pourgette and Davina Douchè (pronounced Dou-shay). They would put on slick shows with tight choreography, working the queens hard but getting pretty good results.

For a long time, Finale had all the best queens, which made a huge dent in Caluzzi's business. Paul Oatham, who owned Caluzzi at the time, was pretty openly gutted about what had happened. He felt like he had been 'shafted' and said that the whole of New Zealand didn't have the audience for two drag venues, let alone two just down the road from each other.

Having had most of their best talent pinched, Caluzzi's shows ended up being seen as a training ground for queens on the road to Finale, which Paul was not happy about. For a while, it felt like this flash new spot was going to extinguish Caluzzi for good. But that was not the case.

Finale's downfall was not a happy one. As often happened when a cast was celebrating a great show, some of the girls were having a little too much fun in the dressing room after their performance. The rumour mill has it that bad backstage habits started affecting the shows and the queens started turning against each other. As the shows began showing some cracks, the venue was hit with some unexpected tax bills and then, seemingly out of nowhere, it abruptly closed in 2012.

Once again, Caluzzi became the crown jewel of K' Road, with some of the city's best queens coming back with their tails between their legs. It turns out the end of Finale wasn't exactly the finale, though.

Arlana teamed up with Macau, the male dancer who'd performed with the queens at Finale, to start up Limelight

Cabaret. They offered the same cabaret-style drag shows but instead of running their own venue, they toured around the city and the country.

I really started to develop a mind for business when Tess brought me in to work at Limelight, after my experience hosting at Switch Bar. All of a sudden, it started to seem possible: maybe I *could* leave my day job and become a professional drag queen full-time.

* * *

Tess had taken me under her wing, and I was quickly learning all the different aspects of being a professional drag queen. From the step up to hosting, to the difference between nightclubs and corporate work, to entertaining smaller groups, to the new world of drag performance that was being showcased on *RuPaul's Drag Race*, working as a drag queen was all about being versatile. If you're versatile, you don't end up at the bottom … and I am a true vers.

Taking ownership of the space and gaining everyone's attention in a club was completely different to moving between small groups of ten, giving each of them a different show in case they'd overheard what you just did for the group next to them.

When I started at Limelight, I was still working selling newspaper subscriptions alongside my sister. At the time,

I thought I was earning decent money, but looking back, I realise I was barely scraping by. I was so good at sales I could pretty much do it in my sleep, which was a good thing as I was out late gigging multiple nights a week. I am still surprised I never fell asleep while I was on a call!

As more opportunities came my way, I started to feel like maybe, with a bit more time and focus, I could make drag my main earner instead of my side hustle. I was determined to become one of the top-tier queens and, while getting the job at Limelight felt like a step in the right direction, I quickly became aware it was not the slick, professional organisation I'd imagined it was.

Because Limelight put on shows at various different venues, each place had to be transformed into a drag space. We wanted the surroundings to be as fabulous as the queens performing within them, but, unfortunately, cost-cutting measures meant this wasn't always the case.

Terrible Photoshopped images of our faces were printed on A4 paper and put under tacky, see-through, plastic mats. The guests often ended up sitting on awful white plastic chairs and, at some shows, they even had to eat off paper plates. The dinnerware was like the stuff we'd used at school camp, and that was not the type of camp our customers were paying for!

The owners had kept the costumes when Finale had closed down, and they were reluctant to get anything new made. This became an issue when I joined, because, at that time, I was huge and I didn't fit any of the outfits they had in their wardrobe. I asked what I was supposed to wear for the group numbers and was told, 'Hey, why don't you just grab whatever you own that is closest to the other costumes? They'll do fine.'

I ended up performing group numbers with the other girls, absolutely nailing the choreography, but still sticking out like a sore thumb because not only was I twice the size of everyone else in the number, I was also wearing some haphazard approximation of their look.

The more shows I did, the more embarrassed I became. It was demoralising to be made to look like the odd one out, and it made me cringe to look out and see people eating with tacky, disposable cutlery.

During my time at Limelight, I'd got on Arlana's good side, so after a show one night, I approached her to run some things past her.

'Look, I love working here and the shows are so much fun, but I think we could really become the biggest thing in drag in this country if we just levelled up in a few ways. For a start, no paper plates. Also, let's get a couple of new costume sets, so we can have two numbers that really wow them, and let's make sure the customers are taken care of as soon as they come in!'

I was full of ideas about how to make everything work.

Arlana was keen. 'You are so right, Kita! I'm totally on board.'

'You got so close to knocking off Caluzzi with Finale,

I think with a few adjustments Limelight could become the top dog!' I added.

After that, I took on a bit more leadership in the company and I got things moving. We had a professional photoshoot so we could stop staring at those god-awful A4 pictures of ourselves on the table. I also offered to update the website and spent hours of my own time working on it.

At every step, Arlana was incredibly supportive, but Macau was resistant to every new idea I had. Even as I continued to do more and more work for the sake of the company, never once asking to be paid for it, he seemed to take my suggestions as criticisms to be talked down to rather than listened to. Even something as minor as simplifying the choreography to make it easier to perform in heels would be enough to send him.

I found myself in a difficult position. Tess had already walked away from the company because it was, as she described it, 'tack-o-rama', and my attempts to make it less 'tack-o-rama' were moving slowly because of one man's pride.

The morning after a particularly exhausting show at Limelight, I was on the toilet when I had an epiphany. There was something about sitting on the dunny, at a time when I felt like I had no energy left inside me, that made me think with a bit more clarity.

I realised that I felt like I was smashing my head against a brick wall trying to make change happen, but nothing was changing and no one appreciated the work I'd been doing.

I messaged Arlana right there and then: 'Thank you for all the opportunities, it's been awesome, but I need to move on.'

I'd gone from the baby of the bunch to one of the most experienced queens they had, alongside other rising stars like Trinity Ice and Anita Wigl'it, but I needed to spread my wings.

Apparently, Macau was gutted. As much as he'd resisted my new ideas, he knew that, since Tess had left, I had become the go-to girl, the most reliable queen on their roster.

It only took a few weeks before I was desperate for somewhere new to perform, so I decided to get in touch with Caluzzi's new owner, Campbell Orr. Campbell had in fact worked at Caluzzi as a bartender, and had bought the bar from Paul. I'd never actually met Campbell, so I sent him a cheeky little message on Facebook:

Hi Campbell Cheesecake Darling [for some reason, at the time I thought it was cute to call people 'cheesecake'],

I've recently handed in my resignation at Limelight Cabaret. After speaking to a few people it was suggested that I should let you know, should you ever need a totally committed, larger-than-life drag queen for anything, I'm a good dancer for a big gurl and can pick up choreography with ease.

Cheers. xx

PS: I'm also totally cool with working to pay off my own uniform (seeing as I'm too slim to fit the other ones!)

At this point, Caluzzi had three queens who would host: Kola Gin, Taro and, of course, the one and only Peena Colada. Taro was about to move to the UK, leaving a huge gap for Caluzzi – a gap, it turned out, that I was just the right size to fill.

I was really surprised when Campbell sent me a short text back: 'I think we could def have a chat.' I could not believe my luck.

We met up for coffee later that week and, before I knew it, I was in. I was hosting nights at Caluzzi!

At first Campbell wanted me to work a solo number, not in the opening number or finale. But the week earlier I'd been added to a Facebook group of Caluzzi girls, and someone had uploaded a video of the latest finale routine. Now, what you need to know is that – in my life outside of drag – I'd never been much of a go-getter. Yes, I'd previously worked my way up a career ladder in a sales role that I didn't love, but inside I was still a lazy teenage boy. Drag was a different story. When I showed up to work on my first night at Caluzzi, I told Campbell I was ready to perform in the finale number. He was shocked.

'How do you know it?'

'I rehearsed it,' I said, 'from a video posted online.'

'Well, you have to do it!' he said with a grin.

The girls next to me onstage that night must have been taken aback at this newcomer who somehow knew every single move.

For a while I was that same giddy, excited newbie, doing everything I could to sparkle and prove to the girls that I could handle the bigger numbers. Caluzzi was well known for being a tightknit family of drag queens, and you couldn't just earn a place in that family overnight. They took me under their wings; we built trust, and I worked hard. It probably helped that – as the jolly, fat old drag queen who could – I wasn't a threat to anyone. (And thankfully, because Peena and I were both hosts, we'd work different shifts and very rarely cross paths.)

One of the girls who left before I arrived had been a bigger girl, although nowhere near my size. She'd left behind a gold sequin outfit that I managed to werk for a short period before our new costumes arrived. A lot of these finale costumes were made without measurements, matching off-the-rack sizing sourced from places like eBay. I felt a bit sorry for the woman sourcing the costumes. She had a hard enough job finding something to suit everyone, and now had the extra hurdle of finding dresses that came in everything from standard size to big-momma. Early on, we ordered me a 6XL dress, and when it arrived it was so tight that I had to wear it as a T-shirt with super high-waisted tights underneath. I must have looked like a potato on two toothpicks, but to be honest none of that affected me. Whenever I was in drag, I had this confidence inside of me where my weight didn't matter.

Mum and Dad with their glowing bundle of joy.

Me at four years old. There are so many things I wish I could tell myself at this age.

My sisters all had flowergirl dresses and I was obsessed with them. They were my absolute favourite feature of my dress-up box. I'm around six years old here, with one of my neighbours, in the early 1990s.

In my early twenties, playing the skins at practice for our band, Whorgy, at my flat in Grey Lynn.

Me and my friend Alesha at a house party in Pakuranga.

My first drag look: no less than iconic Ronald McDonald for a New Year's Eve costume party themed 'Famous', with my friends Richard and Francesca, Grey Lynn, 2009.

Dressed to impress for the very first gig I got when I created a 'drag queen for hire' website, around 2012. It was an *Alice in Wonderland*–themed birthday party.

Me and the magnetic Anita Wigl'it outside Family Bar on K' Road, 2010. We were both brand new on the drag scene, and got on like a house on fire.

When Dad came to visit me and the girls at our drag cabaret bar, Caluzzi, during the Christmas rush of 2017! Featured with his favourite showgirl, Ling Ling.

My day look as
Nick Nash, trying
out electric scooters
for the first time.

A backstage selfie after doing
my makeup in the Caluzzi
dressing room, 2019.

Anita and I strutting our stuff at Wellington Pride, 2019.

Anita and I celebrating the sixth birthday of Kita and Anita's Drag Wars at Phoenix Cabaret, 2019.

Hosting an event at Phoenix Cabaret, 2020.

The dance costume that Elektra Shock made for me, which went on to be featured on *RuPaul's Drag Race Down Under*.

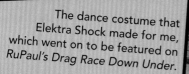

In 2020, thanks to Covid, Caluzzi had to pivot and find new ways to keep the rent paid. Here I am delivering cupcakes to Encore Designer Recycle on Ponsonby Road in Auckland.

NEW ZEALAND DRAG QUEEN
KITA
WWW.KITAMEAN.COM

NEW ZEALAND DRAG QUEEN
KITA
WWW.KITAMEAN.COM

Toot toot, bitches! My lavish purchase of personalised licence plates for my drag mobile.

Out of drag with my drag mother, Tess Tickle, who's got me through so many highs and lows, 2022.

On holiday in Queenstown, New Zealand, with my partner, 2022. As Ru says, 'If you can't love yourself, how in the hell are you gonna love somebody else?'

At Caluzzi, I really began to feel myself. A new era of my career was about to start. I felt like a brand new queen, more sure of myself than ever and ready to leave everything else behind to take drag all the way. I'd also met someone who had quickly become one of my best friends.

*   *   *

I'd met the queen I would come to call Wiggles early on in both of our drag careers, but we never really had a proper conversation. We crossed paths running between shows on K' Road, but we never worked together properly. Then she up and moved to Canada. Good, I thought at the time. It sounded like she was a pretty good performer, and I didn't want her stealing my gigs. After all, there was only room for one campy young queen whose boy name was Nick in my town!

When she returned, I saw her less as competition and more as an opportunity.

I had been booking nights at Switch Bar and was getting pretty good at putting together shows that would pull in crowds. I'd put on a show starring eighteen-year-old Ashley Tonga, who had gone viral singing an amazing version of 'Proud Mary' on *X Factor*, so I put 'As Seen On TV' all over the posters. The place packed out as everyone wanted to see her. She delivered, and I knew I needed to bring in another star to keep the hype going.

When Anita came back to Auckland, she'd just been crowned 'Vancouver's Next Drag Superstar'. It was an amateur competition, similar to Princess to Queen, but I figured if I slapped it on a poster, people would be impressed and intrigued. 'An international award-winner? Sounds like a must-see!'

They flocked to see Anita, and she came through, performing a wicked show that brought the house down.

I started booking her every other weekend at Switch, and, when Tess left Limelight, she was the first person I thought of.

Arlana and Macau were scrambling, but I told them right away, 'Anita Wigl'it is the one. There's no other choice. She loves drag. She has great costumes. She'll have the choreo down really quick. Also, she's a shady bitch with the weirdest smile I've ever seen. She's the real deal. Trust me.'

They trusted me, and pretty soon Anita and I were performing together every weekend, then gossiping late after each show and sharing our dreams for the future.

Anita had seen a show in Vancouver where the girls performing competed against each other, and the audience got to choose who they liked best by tipping them. She reckoned it was just what the Auckland scene needed, and I couldn't have agreed more. She built it up so much: a cut-throat competition in which the best new queens fought hard to win the votes and dollars of the crowd.

'And we could call it … The Big Drag Queen Competition.'

Sometimes Wiggles' ideas need a little bit of adjustment.

'Yeah, or we could call it Kita and Anita's Drag Wars.'

I'm a bit better at coming up with names than she is.

The show that would eventually change our careers started in a pretty unlikely place: an Irish pub called The Dog's Bollix. It was a great little spot near the intersection of Ponsonby Road and Karangahape Road, which had free venue hire, so had seen all sorts of music gigs, comedy shows, twenty-firsts, thirtieths, fortieths and now, for the first time, it would be home to a drag competition.

The format of the show was pretty simple. Anita and I would host, warming up the crowd with the same ruthless banter we had backstage. The audience would then exchange their ticket money for paper tip cash, which they could use to tip the queens as they performed.

At the end of the night, the audience would vote for who they wanted to win on a small piece of paper. We'd count the votes, then the winner would perform again. There were heats and a final, and, later on, we started putting on all-stars shows. The crowds were huge and hungry, and the competition was fierce.

We struck at the right time. *RuPaul's Drag Race* was beginning to creep into mainstream popularity, and, even though you couldn't watch it legally anywhere in New Zealand, plenty of people were torrenting it, chucking it on hard drives and sharing it round.

Now, instead of searching for hours for a good-quality stream without a million pop-up ads, the public could watch queens lip-sync for their lives onstage for just a $10 ticket. An absolute bargain for what quickly became the hottest ticket in town.

I'd put my marketing cap on when we planned how the competition would work. Unlike the Princess to Queen judging panel, the winner of each night of Kita and Anita's Drag Wars was chosen entirely by audience voting. This meant that every competitor would bring along as many friends as they could possibly muster to help increase their chances of winning – and most of their friends were keen.

The culture had changed. When we had started out as drag queens, it definitely wasn't what anyone would describe as cool, but, suddenly, queens were becoming superstars. They were starting to be seen in music videos, movies and ads on TV. Even in New Zealand, a new age of drag popularity was starting and our show was cashing in at just the right time.

We got all sorts at the show, and that was part of the joy. Some queens brought tracks of full Britney Spears medleys, which went way over their allotted time limit, getting every beat of the choreography from the music videos. Others sang live. Some pretended to jizz using silly string. Some learnt painful lessons like 'remember to pin down your wig', and 'throwing glitter actually doesn't look like anything to the audience', and the very important 'don't show your genitals to a crowd who haven't consented'. The shows were wild, but they were also really good!

The buzz grew, and our first ever Drag Wars: All Stars show got moved to Galatos – the very venue where my first-ever drag show had been cancelled. It was a huge venue where legendary bands had performed, and now, our little show had taken off and taken over.

There must have been 500 people there that night. There was a giant banner with our names projected on it, and we had the most bodacious matching outfits with backpacks that had the most expensive ostrich feathers I could find blooming out of them. Members of the media were there to watch, and one of the contestants entered the stage from the back of the room on stilts. The night was iconic, and we knew we really had something.

It still felt early in our drag careers, but we were already becoming what Buckwheat and Tess had been for us. By running this show and giving baby queens stage time in front of hungry crowds, we found ourselves quickly becoming mentors and leaders in the art of drag.

We also found each other to be perfect comedy partners. It was instantaneous; our comedic vibes just clicked from our first show. When we are onstage the zingers just fly. I knew I had found someone I would work with for the rest of my life, and, as fate would have it, our friendship was about to enter into a partnership with much higher stakes.

* * *

Campbell brought all of us Caluzzi girls in one night, and I could tell immediately that we were about to hear bad news. He clearly didn't want to say whatever it was he was about to tell us.

By this time, between Caluzzi, Drag Wars and the occasional night at Family Bar, I had been able to ditch my sales job and devote myself fully to being a working drag queen. Unfortunately, Campbell's announcement was about to throw that life into question.

'Look, girls, running Caluzzi has been my whole life,' he began. 'I do all the accounts, I run the bar, I organise all the shows, I sort out all the advertising … I just have no time for a social life. I have barely been able to spend any time with my husband. I've thought about it long and hard and … it's time for me to sell the business.'

The Caluzzi queens were all in shock.

'Wait, what the actual fuck?'

'What does that mean for us?!'

Campbell reluctantly said, 'I don't know. Look, it's been the greatest joy of my life, running this place, but I've reached my limit. I just don't have it in me anymore. If I could take a small step back and keep it alive, I would, but I just don't think it's possible. I'm telling you girls before anyone else. Please don't tell anyone until it goes public.'

We were all shook.

I immediately thought of Wiggles. At Limelight, Anita and I had talked a lot about our biggest dreams. Drag Wars was one of them, but our other aspiration was to take over Limelight, turn it around, and tour the country as the biggest drag and cabaret company in Aotearoa.

When I left Limelight, we kept talking about starting something new, taking that idea and turning it into a new company, which could outshine both Limelight and Caluzzi. Now it looked like Caluzzi had taken itself out, which neither of us wanted to see.

I didn't know if it was possible, but immediately I thought, 'This could be *our* company.'

After the intensity of the meeting, and as everyone sat around shooting the shit while they waited to open the doors for the night, I sidled up to Campbell and proceeded to plant the seed of an idea to him.

'Hey Campbell, if I knew someone that was going to have a genuine interest in buying this place, would I be allowed to discuss it with them?'

'I don't know who that would be, this is not exactly an investor's dream, but of course,' he replied.

I walked out onto the street and called Wiggles right away. 'Girl, you're not going to fucking believe what has just fallen in our fucking laps. Caluzzi's for sale and we have to buy it!'

Immediately, she was on board.

Anita has always been amazing with money – she saves at the right time, thinks about her spending properly, invests in the right things and she never stops working. Even during the 2021 Auckland lockdown, she got a job stocking shelves at her local supermarket. She's always just hustling to earn some extra cash, which she hardly spends.

My bestie was absolutely ready to go. If only I could have said the same about me.

Unlike Anita, I was an extremely irresponsible spender in my youth. I'd inherited my mother's love of nice things alongside my father's mismanagement of money. I had racked up thousands of dollars on credit cards, spent so much money on cars and stupid fun things, not to mention my own drag, and I had taken out every possible overdraft I could.

I was in massive debt, so when I went into the bank to ask for a $100,000 business loan, I was almost immediately laughed out of the place. I tried every bank I could. I even took my mum along as she had agreed to be guarantor to any loan I might get. Even with her there, ready to be my safety net if things fell through, no one would agree to lend me the money.

We went to each bank and worked through a series of complicated stages in order to ask for the loan, only to be declined, declined and declined once more.

After our final attempt, I was absolutely shattered. The last bank on our list had said no, and it felt like the dream was over. I dropped my mum home, barely able to muster the energy to say goodbye.

As soon as I got home, I hadn't even got out of my car when I collapsed into tears. All my life I had trusted my gut at times like this, and I felt like I knew exactly where I should be going. Buying Caluzzi was exactly what I should be doing, but I couldn't do it – and the reason I couldn't do it was because of my own bad decisions and reckless spending.

I felt heavy with the weight of everyone I was letting down, especially my best mate, Anita, a partner who I had shared this amazing plan with only to be unable to actually follow through with it. I didn't know how I would let her know the bad news.

This was bigger than the two of us as well. In a city with barely any queer spaces, and a limited amount of places for queens to perform, losing Caluzzi was going to have a huge impact on both people's livelihoods and the culture of drag in general. If the experienced queens didn't have a space to perform and earn money, then what hope did the baby queens who were just starting out have? Where could their careers progress to?

I had spent years proving to everyone in my life that this wasn't just some hobby, that it was a career, but I was about to lose the main place where I could actually earn money doing it. All of this, just because I had swiped my cards too much when I was younger. It was all too much. I laid my head on my steering wheel and just wept.

Then my phone rang. I looked down at the screen. It was Mum.

'Sooo, I'm going to do something that your brothers and sisters are going to be absolutely outraged by, but I'm gonna do it because I believe in you.'

She explained she was going to take out a mortgage on the house and give me the cash I needed. I had to pinch myself hard to make sure this was real.

'Pay it back as quickly as you can. But I believe in you, I know you can do it.'

My mother, who I had been separated from for so much of my life, who I had so admired and wanted to spend so much more time with, was giving me the biggest gift I had ever received. To have her see my dream and want to help me get there only made me cry more.

I knew I'd be able to pay her back financially eventually, but I would never be able to truly pay her back for allowing me to take up this opportunity. She had seen the scope of my dream and she wanted to help me get there. What is even more important was that she believed *I* could get there. All the distance we'd had between us over the years felt like it had closed. My mum was instrumental to me making my dreams a reality, to helping me get on the course that would eventually see me become crowned queen on *RuPaul's Drag Race*.

I called Anita.

'We're doing this.'

* * *

Anita and I get on like a House of Drag on fire. We just get each other's jokes, and we get each other's drag. She's been there for me at some of my low points, and when I say low, I mean *really* low.

When I was big, I used to have a huge problem when I did my make-up. The oil-based products I used didn't handle being mixed with any kind of moisture and, unfortunately, it was hard for me not to get moist. If the room I was beating my face in was even close to warm, I would sweat my make-up off, and I would sweat it off fast.

I hate to spoil the illusion of show biz, but in about 95 per cent of the venues I have performed in, the space we were given to get ready in was cramped, hot and uncomfortable. Sweating off my make-up was a massive problem for this massive queen.

It got to the point that, at the short-lived Legend Bar on Karangahape Road, I would actually sneak into the walk-in fridge to finish applying my make-up. People would be like,

'Where's Kita?' and someone would always say, 'That bitch is in the fridge again.'

At the time, I didn't think anything of it. I just thought it was normal and avoided even considering that it might have been a side effect of my weight. I must have been a real spectacle for the bar staff, with my strip of blue mohawk, putting on my clown face in a big fridge.

While the backstage rooms were often too hot, the worst culprits for making me sweat off my make-up were hotel rooms. As Anita and I began working together more frequently, we would often share a room so we could take home a bit of extra cash. When the event organiser was booking the show, we'd tell them to put the money that would have gone into booking us a room each into our fee. That's the sort of thrifty thing that Anita is always thinking about!

We were booked into some dreadful places, and these rooms, girl, they needed air con. We both wanted to shower before we got into drag, and as the shower steamed up, the whole room would heat up. Even if we were lucky enough to have air con, blasting it full-tit still wouldn't bring down the humidity. It was an impossible place for me to put my face on, and, unfortunately, I couldn't quite fit into the mini-fridge to do my make-up.

Anita watched as I took a long time trying to blend everything just right – only to have it slide completely off my face. Every single time it happened, I would have full meltdowns to the point that I'd turn to my sister and say outright, 'Girl, I can't do the gig. It's not going to happen. I can't do the fucking gig!'

The more this happened, the more annoying it got for Anita, so I had started trying to pretend it wasn't happening. Instead, I'd be bubbling up on the inside and that just made me hotter so the make-up would slide right off.

A couple of times, I got so frustrated that I swiped all my make-up products off the table I'd been working at. I went wild.

I take drag so seriously that I never want to walk out in front of people looking like a pile of melted dog shit. Being in drag was one of the few times I felt good about how I looked, and that was being taken away from me by my own sweat.

At those times, I was so lucky to have Anita there to talk me down, and to remind me that we were about to have a lot of fun.

The rooms never cooled down so, instead of getting the perfect blend I wanted to achieve, I'd just end up smearing my make-up onto my face. Anita would tell me that we were in this together, that we would be making each other look good up there. My face might not be perfect but our jokes would be.

I have been so grateful to have her at times like that, and I know she has been just as grateful to have me around. She hasn't had the same make-up problems, and her meltdowns are not as dramatic as mine, but I have helped her with a certain problem involving urination.

She may seem fun and sparkly clean when you see her perform, but that girl is gross. She always talks about how drag padding smells like a toilet, and I always clarify that that might just be *her* pads.

My rule is: you have to get all your wees out before the gig. But Anita always needs to piss during shows, every single time.

Once when we were performing together at Encore Cabaret, she really had to go. At that venue, they had these gorgeous fancy cocktail glasses, and they would always give us whatever we were drinking in those so we felt fancy. Unfortunately, what happened with those glasses means I'll never feel fancy drinking from them again.

Anita was busting and there was no backstage toilet. Even if there had been, getting out of drag is not simple.

She turned to me and said, 'Would it be crazy if I peed in my glass?'

I replied, 'Yes. But go on.'

She got me to guard the door while she stood there pissing into the fanciest glassware they had. While I was blocking the door, some other queens tried to come in but I told them they couldn't.

Then I heard Anita call out, 'Uh, a little emergency ...'

She had filled up her entire glass, so I had to scull the rest of my drink so she had another vessel to pee in.

Onstage, I took the piss out of her all of the time. Backstage, I ended up taking her piss more literally!

That wasn't the only time Anita wasn't able to make it to the toilet. In the wings at the side of a stage, which is pretty much onstage, I've seen her pee into a water bottle. I've watched the door as she peed into a bottle in the middle of Tess Tickle and Buckwheat's incredible drag wardrobe, surrounded by all their expensive stuff. The worst time, though, was definitely backstage at a new venue, Phoenix.

The backstage room at Phoenix must have originally been some kind of outdoor deck that had been closed in. There was this weird gutter on the floor that ran outside and was filled with leaves and things.

On one of the many times when Anita got desperate, she looked at that gutter, turned to me and said, 'That's it. I'm pissing in the trough.'

She'd clearly been eyeing it up since we'd moved into that space, and now she was ready to give it a spin. It was a bad move.

There was so much debris that as she pissed into it, it slowly started filling up until it was in serious danger of overflowing. None of that urine was leaving the room. It couldn't make it past the leaves and rubbish, so it was just sitting there for everyone to see and smell. Eventually, we had to order some drinks from the bar and use those drinks to flush the fucking pee down the drain.

Anita's constant pee antics are distressing, but I am completely complicit in them. I wish I wasn't, but I am. She is my sister and I will always be there to help her when she needs me … even when it involves literal piss.

* * *

Because Wiggles is so amazing with money, we made a bunch of small changes to the way Caluzzi worked, which made a huge difference to the success of the business. When we took it over, the shows were priced at just $59 for a two-course meal and a full show. This was *way* too cheap for what was a five-hour experience. You weren't just watching a show, you had drag queens waiting on your table – it was a fully immersive night.

We wanted to make sure the price was still enticing to audiences, so we offered a three-course meal and bumped the price up by $5, and we added 50 cents to the price of each drink. These were the sort of changes a customer would barely notice, but which made a huge difference to the money coming into our business.

In fact, those small changes were all it took for me to be able to make the money I needed to pay back my mother within just twelve months and become debt-free. That gift from my mother, and Anita's clever business skills, had completely turned my life around.

I could not believe that this was my life. I had to keep reminding myself that what was happening wasn't normal, that I was incredibly lucky to have ended up where I was.

Over the following years our business would grow, my drag journey would start to explode, I'd get on TV – and I'd end up in a relationship so toxic it threatened to take it all away. Life was about to become a real roller coaster.

CHAPTER 9

House bound

KITA AND ANITA'S DRAG Wars quickly developed into a beast that could no longer be contained within the walls of The Dog's Bollix. As welcoming as the venue had been, it didn't have enough room for our performers to change and prepare, and the audience was bursting at the seams. Fortunately, there was another venue that wanted to tempt us into their arms.

When Finale had fallen over, it had left in its wake an amazing venue for putting on shows, and that opportunity was leapt on by a company called Encore. Rather than being focused solely on drag, Encore was a cabaret company. They had showgirls, musical theatre numbers and MCs in suits, and they offered the old-school type of dinner theatre. The space was perfectly set up for drag shows – after all, just a few years earlier that was what it had been created for.

They saw that our show was booming and made us a pitch: we bring the show to their venue, which was all ready to go with a high stage, flash lights and heaps of room for a crowd, and we keep the ticket money while they keep the bar money. It was a great deal, and we were pretty happy to be leaving a venue that was named after a canine's balls.

We quickly became a staple at Encore. And not just a staple, we were soon the most popular show they had. There would be lines down the street and the amount of cash going over the bar was massive.

When Encore moved up the road to a bigger venue, which was even better kitted out for big stage productions, and rebranded as Phoenix, Drag Wars grew again. There was almost no standing room left in the entire venue, and the crowd wasn't just the mates that contestants were bringing to ensure they got plenty of votes. There was buzz about the show and all sorts of people were coming to check it out – even the straights!

We soon realised that the money they were making over the bar from our show was paying Phoenix's rent for the rest of the week, and we were once again in a position to make a big business move.

Caluzzi was packed out every week, and we were constantly having to turn away many of the lucrative (and often outrageous) hen parties that we didn't have room for. We'd even had to start adding mini-shows at 6 pm, at which a drag queen would host the hen party with cheeseboards and games before the main show. Even though we weren't giving them the full experience, we still had to turn parties away every week.

We realised that if we could take over Phoenix, we could have multiple shows running on the same night and not lose any business.

Anita and I went to meet with the owners of Phoenix and put our case to them. Two of the owners agreed to sell to us right away, but one still believed in the cabaret venue she had poured so much blood, sweat and tears into. Her name is Zarlene, and she is now our business partner.

With her help we started to fill the calendar with all sorts of events. While we've added more drag shows, we've also had bingo and paint-and-sip nights hosted by queens; we've had queer comedy shows; we've hosted a fundraiser for Auckland Central's Green member of parliament, Chlöe Swarbrick; and we've even had New Zealand music legend Ladi6 do a concert there.

Anita and I are now running not one but two venues devoted to drag performance on Karangahape Road. They are packed to the brim multiple nights a week and they've seen iconic young queens go from their first-ever drag performances to appearing on television. Make sure you come visit if you are ever in Tāmaki Makaurau, and if Zarlene serves you at the bar, be extra nice to her because she is the best.

Our little live show that was once a dream in Anita's head had blown up, and it was soon to take a jump to a whole other level – Drag Wars was headed for the (laptop) screen!

* * *

At one of the first shows we did at Encore, something major happened. We got … I guess you would call it … scouted. 'Entertainment scout' might make you think of some big Hollywood man in a white suit who drives a Cadillac and whisks you off to the big smoke, but our scout was so not that. Instead, she was a short girl with dyed hair and glasses, who I now love with all of my heart.

Amanda Pain is one of the most cherished people in my life. She was the one who got everyone at my *Drag Race* finale party to put their phones in a bag so no one could spoil the ending. Since we first met at Phoenix, she's been with me for some of my highest highs and my lowest lows, from when I've been inconsolably crying, to when I've been bragging up a storm and needed someone to take me down a peg or two. She's a huge part of why I am where I am today, and it all started when she saw Anita and I hamming up a storm hosting Drag Wars.

She'd seen a little bit of my act once before, at a show by season six *Drag Race* winner, Bianca Del Rio, at which I was lucky enough to be one of the opening acts. Amanda was a huge fan of *Drag Race* and Bianca brought her onstage that night and made her life. As a producer at Warner Brothers, she knew she wanted to make a TV show that showcased drag from our corner of the world. She must have liked my act enough to follow me on social media, and when she saw a post about Drag Wars, she headed along to Encore, where she saw the seeds of the show she had been dreaming about.

Amanda had been badgering her big boss about making a drag TV show for months but kept being told that there wasn't enough talent in little old Aotearoa to cast such a thing. That night, she watched us hurling zingers at each other at our usual Energizer-Bunny speed in between the immense talent of the amateur drag stars competing, and she saw it. She took a video and sent it to her boss with a note that said, 'I think we have our hosts.'

Almost immediately she got a response. He loved what he saw, and he was ready to put a pitch together for TVNZ.

* * *

When I woke up one morning to see an email from Warner Brothers, I definitely did not believe it. I was like … *The* Warner Brothers? Like, from *Animaniacs*? I was sure it was some kind of scam. But it wasn't a scam. The email was addressed to me and they definitely did know who I was and they definitely weren't trying to get me to transfer money to a prince in a foreign country or sell me penis enlargement pills.

It wasn't quite *Animaniacs* Warner Brothers, but Warner Brothers New Zealand, who almost exclusively make reality TV and are behind all the biggest reality shows that air on TV here. The email said:

> We have a vision for a programme that puts the spotlight
> on New Zealand drag artists and we want you to be a part
> of it. We'd like you to come in for a meeting so we can
> talk ideas.
> Kind Regards,
> Amanda Pain
> Producer
> Warner Brothers NZ

After everything that had been happening with Anita and my burgeoning drag empire, I couldn't believe that more good news had come my way. I pinched myself so hard it left a mark.

I sent a super-professional email back:

> Yes, yes, yes, FUCKING YES, a thousand times yes. Super
> fucking keen. Let's have a meeting.
> Kita x

We had a meeting with Amanda and some other members of the team at Warners, and the brief was open. They knew they wanted a drag show, they knew they wanted us hosting it, but they wanted to know about the show *we* wanted to make.

I went away, hammered through some of my weirdest and wildest ideas and came back with a pitch that merged two of my favourite shows: *Big Brother* and *RuPaul's Drag Race*.

I have loved reality TV ever since the first season of *Survivor* aired. Then when I saw *Big Brother* I could not believe how good it was. It was perfect: like *Survivor* but in a house and with penises after hours. It was my little gay fantasy show, and now, years later, I wanted to combine it with my big gay fantasy show.

We wanted to have drag artists living in a house together. They'd be filmed 24 hours a day and made to do stupid challenges. They'd scheme together to sabotage each other's performances, they'd fight, they'd party and, who knows, maybe we would even get a little romance in the mix. Of course, Anita and I would live in the house with them, drinking, partying and bossing them round. It would be all-out chaos and unlike anything else on TV.

We took our concept to the producers and they loved it … but they definitely couldn't make it.

The thing was, they wanted us to make a web series with fifteen-minute episodes. They didn't have the budget to set up cameras all around a house, film 24 hours a day and then have a team of editors trawl through all of the footage to try to make a show.

We had to scale our dreams back, but after years of pulling together stage shows with looks from op-shops and Trade Me, we were pretty good at being thrifty and working with what was available.

While we couldn't live our full *Big Brother* fantasy, *House of Drag* took elements of that pitch and made them into a much more streamlined, easier-to-film show. Our contestants did live in a house together, but, despite our desire to shack up and party with them, Anita and I stayed in our own homes.

Each day, we'd be driven out to the House of Drag, where we'd do a little sketch by ourselves, give them a challenge, make them compete in the drag room, get the winner to choose a bottom two and then we would choose one of the bottom two to have their light dimmed and be told to 'Da da da-da da, FUCK OFF!' (This was our trademarked catchphrase. Well, it's not actually trademarked but if you steal it, I will fight you.)

Our onscreen discussion about who would go home was a ridiculous game of word association, which was a little throwback to my Theatresports days, and it gave even the toughest eliminations a fun bit of silliness. Eventually, one winner would take home $10,000, a TV and some free broadband. We were sponsored by a broadband company, just in case that seems like an odd prize. It is important for a queen to have internet – especially in these strange times!

We got to be super involved with the process, with the Warners team trusting that we knew the Kiwi drag scene and what sort of show would help showcase it the best. It barely felt like any time had passed since we'd been apprentices to amazing legends like Buckwheat and Tess Tickle, but here we were, in a position to be seen as leaders to young drag artists, helping put together the cast for the first-ever drag reality show filmed in Aotearoa. We were honoured to be heading up such a monumental moment in our little country's drag history.

Now, I will be the first to admit that it wasn't the slickest, most fabulous production that's ever been created. It was very, very far from that. The show was hastily made with a small budget, and, to make it financially viable, we shot the whole thing in a matter of days. The contestants would be filmed getting ready for one episode's challenge, while Amanda and I were hastily writing the script for the acting challenge to be filmed the next day. The drag room the contestants had to perform in was tiny, and we had no option to go overtime because the mansion had been booked to house the shoot for *The Bachelor* or *The Bachelorette* or *Bachapalooza* or whatever show was coming in next.

We made do with the resources we had, and we were proud of our little drag show. The show got lapped up by a small but passionate audience, and it brought attention to some of the amazing kings and queens in New Zealand, and me and my bestie Wiggles got to do a lot of silly stuff together. We got to showcase drag kings, AFAB (assigned female at birth) queens and hyper queens, and we got them to do all sorts of challenges from rap battles, to dressing up as animals, to hosting drag bingo.

But it wasn't always easy.

* * *

While Kita and Anita were shown to be the all-powerful hosts of *House of Drag*, running the show and making the brutal decisions about which drag artists made it and, therefore, occupying a different level to the drag stars competing, that wasn't necessarily our position in the drag hierarchy outside of the show.

We had only been hosting Drag Wars for a few years, and we didn't really consider ourselves to be mentors yet. We were both barely 30, and many of the queens on the show were only a little younger than us. In fact, some of them had been rising in the scene at the same time as we had.

There were several eliminations that felt quite painful. Shavorn Abörealis went home at the end of season one, episode one. She is a funny, fierce, capable queen, who has all the skills to make it big in the drag world, but someone had to go home first and Shavorn had failed in the first photo challenge. Maybe if we'd started with a different challenge, she would have been that week's winner, but it wasn't to be. I'm gutted that the viewers didn't get to see more of her talent, though.

While it was sad to see her go, I don't think it has dimmed her star in the long run. Ever since then, she has showed such a massive devotion to drag, and her craft has got better and better. I have a feeling we might see her on a much bigger platform sooner rather than later.

The toughest elimination was in the third episode of season one, when Trinity Ice was sent home. She is my drag sister. We'd come up together, working in all the same venues and putting on shows, but above all that she had also been my flatmate for years! She is truly one of my best friends.

When she left – and she had to go as she'd designed a truly dogshit dress – I was inconsolable. I immediately burst into tears as it just felt so horrible to send my sister packing. But I wasn't allowed to cry. A producer pulled me aside and told me I had to sort myself out. We needed to appear as if we were above the competitors. It didn't matter what our relationships were before the show, we were the hosts here. As a result, we had to reshoot the elimination to show me being as cold as ice and not shedding a single tear. I knew it was better for the show, but it did not feel good at all.

As soon as filming wrapped, we were all friends. We'd hang out on the couches, shooting the shit, still friends who knew that this was nothing personal, that we just had a show to make.

There was so much to be proud of across both seasons of the show. In the incredible Hugo Grrrl, we were able to crown the first drag king to win a drag competition TV show anywhere in the world. Since being on the show, he has continued to grow his own empire, putting on dozens of shows a year, doing corporate work, MCing events all over Wellington, Auckland and beyond, and even writing and starring in a drag theatre show for kids at the prestigious Circa Theatre.

In the second season, we had two AFAB queens competing, one who identified as straight at the time the series aired, sparking lots of conversations about inclusion within the drag community. Yeh, we did it long before Maddy Morphosis.

That season, we crowned Spankie Jackzon, a queen based in little old Palmerston North, who represented drag in its most brash Kiwi form. We also got to showcase the incredible, versatile talents of Elektra Shock, and anyone who saw what she did on our show would not have been surprised to see her make it so close to the finale on *Drag Race Down Under*. We also got a bit of extra cash for season two, so Anita and I could pop over to Thailand and get some upgraded costumes, which ruled.

While getting the chance to compete on *Drag Race* was a dream come true, there was something truly special about the opportunity given to us with *House of Drag*. Anita and I were able to not just host the show and hog a decent chunk of the run time with our opening sketches, but we were also part of the development and casting of the show. We got to make the little Kiwi drag show that could and I'll never stop being proud of that. Maybe one day we'll get another few bucks from TVNZ to churn out a third season, but until then I will cherish the memories I have of playing up for the cameras in the *House of Drag*.

It was a busy time in my life, but while my professional life was rocketing, in my personal life, I was spiralling. I had got myself into a truly toxic relationship, and as glam as I felt on my TV set, I was feeling smaller than ever when the drag came off.

* * *

My love story, if you can call it that, with Noah began the same way many gay relationships do – with a Grindr message. Noah lived down south, but he was in Auckland often, and, even though he identified as straight, when he was in town he was always looking to hook up with trans girls or feminine boys. I fit the latter of those categories, so on one of those trips we had hooked up.

At that stage in my life, I always used drag photos in my dating app profiles. It was the only time I felt beautiful, and I was scared to put my actual face out there. It also helped me avoid hooking up with the type of gays who couldn't cope with boys who dressed as girls for a living.

Noah was six foot three, Māori and he played rugby. He was basically everything I dreamed of in a man. We had fun together.

Then something strange happened. He said he had a dog that was ill, and he needed some help paying the vet bills. He kept reinforcing to me how important the dog was to him, and how devastated he'd be if the dog passed away. He told me he needed $1000 to pay the vet.

At the time, I was making decent money at Caluzzi and I wanted to pay some of that forward, so I thought, 'Why not?' I gave him the money and didn't think of it again. After that, we messaged each other from time to time, but I didn't see him again for a long time.

Slowly, through our messages, I started to work out what had happened. The dog story had been a sort of half-truth. There *had* been a dog involved, but it wasn't a family pet. It wasn't even a dog he had met. It was a racing dog, which had lost a race, and he owed someone serious money from betting on it. At least, I think that's what happened – to be honest with you I am still not quite sure.

Having had a glimpse into what had actually happened, I had no qualms about wanting my money repaid and hit him up to give me the cash back. I got no response. I hit him up again. When I got no reply a second time, I figured he was bad news and decided to cut him out of my life. If he wouldn't give me my money back, what was the point in keeping in touch?

More than a year later, he messaged me completely out of the blue. Noah had grown up in a deeply conservative family and they had found some photos and messages on his phone and some things from his search history that alluded to what he had been getting up to when he visited Auckland. They'd kicked him out, so he'd driven straight up to Auckland and he had nowhere to stay.

Given he'd already scammed me out of money, I decided not to tell him to come to my house. Instead, we met at a local park. He showed up with his tail between his legs, apologising over and over for having taken my money. Then he explained what had happened with his family. It turned into this amazing, vulnerable confession about who he was, his background, his faith and his love for his whānau, who he was desperate not to let down. He had no idea what to do, but he was upset to the point that he was considering ending his own life.

Apart from a few stray messages, we hadn't really spoken in a year, but I still wanted to help him. His situation sounded awful and I didn't want him to be stuck in Auckland with nowhere to stay. His plan had been to sleep in his car that night, but there was no way I was letting that happen.

I said, 'Come on, drive to mine. I'll get you some dinner and you can stay with me for as long as you need.' I had no idea how long that would be.

The fabulous Wellington drag queen Felicity Frockaccino was staying at my house at the time, so when Noah was added to the mix, the house began to feel really full. It was a one-bedroom apartment, which was now housing three people, two of whom were drag queens who needed a lot of space for their outfits.

I thought maybe Noah would be there for one night, but after a week, he was still there. When Felicity left, he stayed on. Of course he did – I was giving him shelter, I was feeding him, and I was giving him a pretty comfortable life compared to the tumultuous home he had left down south.

Pretty soon, we were in a relationship. In some ways, it felt like I had won the lottery. I had never really felt attractive to anyone. I was this obese man with shaved eyebrows and crazy hair, and I worked full-time as a drag queen. I had convinced myself that no one could ever love me, and that was what I deserved. So, when this guy came into my life and started showing me affection, it was unlike anything I had ever felt before. To be able to just lie in each other's arms, to kiss someone on the regular ... it was something I never thought would happen for me.

I helped Noah start his life in Auckland and got him set up with a job. I spoke to my friend Hans, who headed up the security team at Family Bar. Hans has since passed, but he was an incredible man with the warmest heart, who always took such good care of the queens.

Hans was kind enough to give Noah a job on the door at the club. I was so happy to get him that job, but it gave me an early sign that things were not going to go as well as I had hoped between us. Noah was great at the job, but he didn't want anyone there to know we were living together or that we were together at all.

Even though I had brought him into the amazing Family Bar, my second home, I felt I had to do his bidding. I would say 'hi' to him on my way in, as if he was any other security guard. In fact, I was even less friendly to him than I was to the other security guards.

For the entirety of our relationship, affection between us only ever took place at home. While Noah was embarrassed to be seen with me, he was not embarrassed to ask me to do things he knew would hurt me just to save his face. He would get me to walk ahead of him when we went out, so that it wouldn't look like we were even friends, let alone a couple. We would go on dates, but he would never so much as put a hand on my back, let alone kiss me in front of anyone else. It was horrific, and, while I was used to feeling alone and freakish when I was out in town, this brought on a whole new level of shame. It made me feel worthless.

When we were alone, though, it was a different story. He'd tell me he loved me, he'd shower me with affection, he'd make me feel like the most important and beautiful person in the world – which is why I was always happy to hand him my credit card when he asked for it.

He would say he needed money for groceries and then go out for hours. When I got my bank statements, I learnt that he'd been using my money to gamble. Each time, he had headed straight to the local TAB betting shop.

I would never push him too hard about the money. In fact, I added to the problem by buying him things. I'd get him expensive cell phones, flash sneakers, beautiful cologne … Even though, a lot of the time, he made me feel like nothing, those few times when he made me feel so loved made me want to shower him with gifts. Unfortunately, the love I showed to him was not returned.

Eventually, he reconciled with his family and moved back in with them. After that, he would come up to Auckland for weekends and even then he spent most of the time with his friends.

On one particularly bad night, he bought all his friends ecstasy, but never paid the dealer for it. He ended up being chased by a whole bunch of gang members, who threatened to beat him up and leave him on the street if he didn't cough up the money for the drugs … so he called me. I got up, got dressed and went to rescue the man who, a year into our relationship, wouldn't even let me call him my boyfriend.

At home one day, he asked to borrow my credit card so he could go and buy some groceries. Despite his history, and how he had abused my trust time and time again, I handed it over. After he'd been gone far too long for a trip to the supermarket, I checked my bank balance. Five thousand dollars was gone. It had been withdrawn at the TAB, where I was certain he'd already gambled most of it away. I was done. I decided it was time to confront him.

He had taken my car, so I had to take an Uber down to the betting shop. When I showed up, I could tell from the look on his face he had not been expecting to see me. He tried to explain that he owed some people money, but I wasn't hearing it. The $5000 he'd withdrawn had already dwindled down to $3000, and now he was begging me to let him take out another $4000 to help him win more. I couldn't believe that he had the gall to ask me for *more* money. He hadn't even got any groceries, and we really needed some eggs.

When we got home, I tried to tell him I was done, but he started crying and said people were chasing him for the money. He said he was scared for his life. I wish I could say I stayed strong, but – once again – I just continued to ply him with money and gifts.

It took me so long to realise just how unhappy he was making me. Not only was he rinsing me for cash, but he was also draining me of my confidence. Even though we had a physical relationship, he still made incredibly shocking comments. He told me my weight was off-putting, he said how I looked was a turn-off … and I let him.

I would come home from amazing days on set filming the reality TV show I had helped conceive, to have someone tell me I was not worthy of their love and affection. It's hard to reconcile what was going on in my personal life with how my work life was going at the time. It is like I was two different people. I was a business owner, one of the most booked people in my field of work, and yet here I was stuck in a relationship that was making a serious dent in my personal and financial worth. At work, I was evolving into my own brilliant, confident version of myself, but I was also holding myself back by pouring so much of my energy into someone in my home life who only took from me.

I realise now that I was not the only person who was a victim of his gambling. His addiction got so bad that he pawned off family heirlooms to pay his debts. The possibility of winning big on the horses … or the dogs … or the rugby … was all-consuming and caused him to make bad decisions constantly. That's what addiction can do. It was a real problem that he had, a medical issue, and I have no judgement for anyone who goes through that. I, myself, am susceptible to the thrill of gambling and have to keep very strong boundaries to stop myself from succumbing to it.

After almost two years together, I finally broke it off with Noah. Exactly what the final straw was I don't know, it might have been a harsh comment or him stealing from me again. It was a hard decision to make as this was the closest thing I had ever had to a true romantic relationship.

He'd come into my life at a time when drag was 99.9 per cent of my life, and he'd provided my one reprieve from that life. I allowed him to treat me poorly because I didn't want to lose the one non-drag thing I had.

I'd been saving money and preparing to buy us a house. That's what I wanted for us – the happily-ever-after fantasy – but I knew it wasn't doing me any good, and I knew I deserved better. I left him, and then made one of the biggest decisions of my entire life.

* * *

The decision to get a gastric bypass happened over a couple of days. My relationship with Noah had made me realise how little value I placed in myself. I felt like I didn't deserve love and affection, and my weight was a huge part of why I felt that way.

For the first time in my life, I had money in the bank, not just enough to get by on each week but a decent amount that I'd been putting aside to buy a house. It was then that I decided that before I bought a house, I wanted to stop looking like one.

I'd never even considered a gastric bypass before and suddenly my gut was telling me 'go to Thailand – get the surgery!' So I thanked my gut for her services and, two months later, I was on a plane to make her smaller.

Honestly, it was the easiest thing I've ever done in my life. I didn't feel good right after the surgery, though. I felt like I'd been hit by a train. Luckily for me, I have a secret skill that always comes in handy at times like this. Whenever I'm in a bad way, I'm able to shut my eyes and immediately go to sleep. It's like my superpower, but instead of helping to fight crime, it has helped me get over some of my worst hangovers.

After the surgery, I used my superpower and I decided to just shut my eyes and sleep. And sleep I did. I was out for about 24 hours. It was great news for my recovery, but not such great news for my family and friends.

Everyone back home knew that I had taken off overseas, and they had the time and date of my surgery written down. When they didn't hear from me for more than a day after I'd gone under the knife, they freaked out.

When I finally woke up, I had so many emails, missed calls and texts. The one from Mum was pretty indicative of all of them:

> Nick – please call me back! We're all so worried. Just let us know you're ok. I have the page open to book flights. Just call me, please. Mum.

My reply:

> Sorry, I was snoozing!

Within three days of the surgery, I was back up walking and drinking water again. I recovered so quickly that they sent me back to my hotel early. I'm not saying my experience is how it would be for anyone else, but for me it was a super-fast recovery. I felt fine, and the results came soon after for me.

During the surgery, they removed a big part of my stomach, and because there was less room, I physically couldn't eat the way I used to. The weight just shed from me, and I've never looked back.

I got the surgery done right after we filmed the second season of *House of Drag*, but the show wasn't released until over a year later. By the time I watched the show, I'd not only had the surgery but I'd also been living in my new body for what felt like a seriously long time. Then there I was on screen, the bigger version of me, being seen each week as if that was what I looked like now. It was completely surreal, but it was also a good reminder for me of the transformation I had been through and why I'd done it. It made me even more certain of the decision I'd made and encouraged me to keep going.

The surgery is not a permanent solution. As time moves on, it becomes easier to eat more and, if you don't eat right and exercise, the weight can start to creep back on.

As season two of *House of Drag* aired, New Zealand moved into its first level four Covid-19 lockdown. While I was stuck at home, it would have been very easy to fall into my old habits and just start eating absolute shit again, but seeing myself on screen helped me acknowledge the journey I was on and encouraged me to keep persevering. I'll be the first to admit, I'm still not exercising as much as I should – and I should, because the more I work out, the more exquisite snacks I'll be able to eat.

While I was on TV (well, TV on the internet) every week, my actual career was at a standstill. All live performances had been cancelled, and they wouldn't return for months. Both Phoenix and Caluzzi had to close their doors and, sadly, drag queens were not deemed an 'essential service', so I was scraping by on my savings and the few gigs that took place over Zoom.

When we first went into lockdown, I felt so pessimistic that I spiralled completely. I was convinced that we would lose everything, that the venues would have to shut and that I would have to sell all my favourite and most expensive pieces of drag just to get by. To anyone who tried to tell me otherwise, I would just say, 'Nah girl, it's done. It's over.'

I was convinced that I was going to lose everything, and that when we were eventually allowed out I'd have to take a job at a call centre.

Thanks to Aotearoa's incredible pandemic response, we were back on our feet pretty soon, and, not long after that, I got the phone call that would change my life forever and that probably led you to pick up this book.

* * *

It was November 2020 when I first heard the news. I was in Queenstown with Anita and we were sitting in the Skyline gondola heading up to perform at a corporate event when I got a call from Amanda. I could tell it was urgent. She sounded so excited.

'Have you heard? This is so so so top secret. But you might have heard. They're doing *Drag Race Down Under* and they're filming it here. *Drag Race* is coming to New Zealand. And they want to see tapes from both of you!'

As good as things in my life had been getting, I never in a million years expected to be auditioning for the actual RuPaul herself. This was next level – more than I had ever dreamed. Our little country hosting a local version of the best TV show ever made – and I might get to be part of it? How was all of this happening to me? I felt so happy and so full ... that said, it was pretty soon after my surgery, so I felt full all of the time.

CHAPTER 10

Entering the drag Olympics

IT WAS ABOUT THREE weeks after that first heads-up that I had to send my audition tape in for the Olympics of drag. *RuPaul's Drag Race* first screened in the United States in 2009, and the show has been largely responsible for bringing the art of drag into mainstream entertainment. Hosted by legendary queen RuPaul, *Drag Race* features queens competing in front of celebrity judges across a number of weeks to win the title of 'America's next drag superstar' – and before long, 'Thailand's/ the UK's/Canada's/Holland's next drag superstar', and, we hoped, soon, 'Down Under's next drag superstar'.

Every day, I would bug Amanda and everyone else I knew at Warner Brothers, but there were no extra titbits of information for us to gobble up. Even though it had sounded like Anita and I would be sure things for the show, each day when we didn't hear anything made me worry that maybe they'd skip out on us and, instead, fill the cast with flashier Aussie queens.

I knew that ultimately everything in *Drag Race* was decided by RuPaul herself. No matter what anyone thought or suggested, if Ru didn't like my vibe, I would not be on the show.

As it was *RuPaul's Drag Race Down Under*'s first season and as was the case with the other international spin-offs, the production team had a fair idea of who they wanted in the cast from the outset. The standard approach to auditioning for *Drag Race* is to send a big video package that introduces you and really showcases your talents, as well as your prospective Snatch Game character. (During Snatch Game, contestants choose a celebrity to impersonate on a mock game show.)

I didn't do a full audition reel. In fact, what I did was extremely casual. I just sent a video of me, out of drag, saying hello to Ru, introducing myself and explaining what my drag was all about. I felt confident, but I had no way of knowing exactly how I could impress anyone with this simple video, which was a bit like a dating profile.

From what I've heard through the grapevine, a few people got an immediate 'yes' from the queen herself. As for me, I made it through to the second round of auditions, which involved having a Zoom call, in drag, with one of the producers. During the call, they asked me more questions about what I was all about and what I could bring to the show. Again, I felt confident, but, as the days went by, it was hard not to replay every moment over and over. Had I laughed enough? Had I laughed too much? Had I looked like I didn't love drag enough? Had I looked like I loved drag too much?

I still don't know if what I went through was the same process as everyone else. I've never talked to Anita or Elektra about their auditions. I do know there were a couple of other Kiwi queens who got to the Zoom stage of the process but didn't make the cut.

What I have heard, and this excited me almost as much as being cast, was that Ru had watched some of *House of Drag*, and apparently it was Elektra's impressive run on our show that meant she got the chance to audition for the big one.

As casting was happening, there was an extra pressure that was stressing me out a lot: what if Anita got cast and I didn't?

Ever since we'd started hosting together a few short years earlier, we had always been linked. We work so well as a pair, we've always helped boost each other up and we have always been there for each other. This has led to us constantly being seen as a unit, and I think both of us have wanted to be able to step out on our own sometimes. Of course, we want to keep working together, and we will 'til our pubes turn grey, but the advent of *Drag Race* brought with it the opportunity for us to branch out as individuals. It was an exciting opportunity, but a scary one. It felt a bit like the question of who was the better member of the duo was about to be decided by the casting of a TV show.

If only one of us had got on the show, the other would immediately become her sidekick. As this was the first season of *Drag Race Down Under*, what if Anita got on and I didn't … and then there was no season two? She would forever be the TV star and I would be … the other one.

After the Zoom interview, it took a few weeks before we got confirmation towards the end of November 2020: Anita and I were both on. Finally, I could stop overthinking things. Now, all I had to worry about was what would actually happen on the show.

Elektra had started working at Caluzzi just a few months before we got the confirmation, so we knew she was on too. Obviously, the three of us had to pretend to be surprised to see each other when we entered the werk room on the show, but no one could work as closely together as we do and keep that secret. After all, we'd taken the exact same three weeks off work!

Drag Race Down Under would start shooting in Auckland at the end of January 2021. We were so excited, but it didn't leave much time to sort all our outfits. The hustle was on.

* * *

I had heard that when you get cast on *Drag Race*, they send you a list of all the outfits you need to assemble pretty quickly. In our case, though, it wasn't that quick. There was a pretty substantial stretch of time during which I knew I was going to be on the show but I didn't have any idea about the sort of looks I needed to prepare.

Each episode features a main challenge, such as Snatch Game, then a runway, which involves creating a themed look. Both the challenge and the runway have weight when it comes to the judging, but whatever your take on the theme is can drive you to a win or send you crashing to the bottom.

A few times during the season, we might have to construct the look on the day, but for most runways, we would be utilising the drag we'd brought with us based on a list provided before shooting started.

I knew I wanted good stuff, and good stuff takes time, so, even though I didn't have the list of themes, I immediately got to work getting designers to put together some pieces for me, and I went shopping for some pieces myself and constructed what I could.

I knew I'd need some dance costumes, which thankfully I already had, and I knew there would be a finale look. This meant I could get ahead on a couple of outfits, but when the list arrived it contained a few curveballs.

Some of the themes ended up being a little different from what I'd read on that sheet, but most of them, like 'Sea

Sickening: show us your fiercest ocean drag', were exactly as they'd been written.

We were even given a couple of suggestions for what we might do. For example, for Sea Sickening, they suggested maybe a mermaid look or a scary creature from the sea. (Once again, my love of Ursula from *The Little Mermaid* came into play here.)

For that theme, they also said the focus would be on accessories. This added a bit of stress while we put those looks together, but it seemed to have been pretty much forgotten once we took to the stage. I built a twisted crown covered in rhinestones so I could meet the accessory brief, but a lot of the other queens didn't have anything. Art Simone had also accessorised with a bunch of extra pieces, but after she looked around at how few other queens had fulfilled that part of the brief, she ditched her extra jewellery and walked the runway in the accessory-less form of her look.

Some of the wonderful items I sourced before I got the list didn't see the light of the runway stage, but many of them came in handy. One outfit I had been designing with a costume maker in Thailand was a metallic bodice with a matching light-up pigtail wig. I knew it was cool, but I wasn't sure it would fit any of the themes.

When I got the list, there was no 'Club Kids', no 'Futuristic', no 'Robot' theme – all of which had featured on previous *Drag Race* shows. I was worried I'd spent a huge amount of money for nothing. But then I looked again and saw 'headdress' on the list. I thought, 'Yeah, that will work. Part of it goes on my head and that's enough.'

While preparing my own looks, I couldn't stop myself from helping my fellow Kiwis. I was Elektra's boss, so I knew exactly what she had in her drag wardrobe and I knew it wouldn't be enough for the show.

I said to her, 'Look, girl, apart from the stuff I need, you take whatever you want from my closet.'

I tried to push my stuff on her, offering her all the drag I had. Maybe she didn't think it would fit well or maybe she wanted to sort it on her own, but she didn't take many things – not even tights. She did take a bunch of wigs and a couple of gowns, though. I was happy to help her out a bit!

I knew Anita would be well kitted out for her drag, but I also knew that a big part of the show was what we would wear when we were out of drag.

More and more on the show, queens have been putting effort into turning out boy looks that match their drag personas, and while old Wiggles has some fabulous drag looks, I knew that what she wore out of drag was – to be frank – boring as fuck, so I bought her some more colourful, fun stuff online and she looked great on the show. Then she sold it all for profit on Depop after the show … shady bitch!

* * *

Apart from my Kiwi sisters Anita and Elektra, one of the only people who knew I was off to *Drag Race* was my mum. Every time a new look was finished, I would show it off to her and she would be absolutely gagged. She was also the person I talked to about my deepest fears going into the show.

I was terrified that I would go home first, and I knew if that happened I would come home emotionally devastated. Mum would try to cheer me up by giving me positive affirmations at every turn. She would say to me, 'I know it's scary, Kita, but out of all these people, you got on the show! That's something to be proud of.'

I had to pinch myself that this was my mum, from whom I'd been so distant in the past, championing me every step of the way. I felt so lucky to have her support me unconditionally and just be in my corner. And she was right, of course. The fact that I was one of the ten people picked *was* massive. But if I went home first, I'd always be the queen who went home first – and that sticks.

As she coached me through those early anxieties, it was almost like my real mother had become my drag mother.

But while *those* two worlds collided, I still hadn't reconciled Nick Nash with Kita Mean. For so long, drag had been a kind of freedom from my body and self-judgement. I knew we'd have to be on camera in and out of our looks, and even though I'd had the gastric surgery, I still didn't feel like I could just flick a switch from Nick to Kita and back again. I worried that other queens who were more comfortable and confident in themselves would make me look like a fraud. Who was the real Kita?

The one other person who knew where I was during filming was my sister Trinity Ice. Apart from working together all the time, she was also living in my house during the shoot. Fortunately, she loves keeping a secret and I think holding that knowledge made her feel superior. She loved strolling around gigs knowing something the other girls didn't know.

For a while, I thought my secret was completely safe, but, unfortunately, the *Drag Race* filming dates clashed almost exactly with the dates for Auckland Pride. In the initial Pride festival announcement, Kita and Anita were booked and blessed and all over the shows, and our names were in big letters on all of the posters – then suddenly, we were scrubbed from all the Pride promotional material. It was the first year in many that I'd gone without performing at Big Gay Out, a huge all-ages Pride event that happens in a beautiful Auckland park, and I was gutted about that.

People definitely knew something was up, and for a while, it felt like everyone I knew was asking me about it. I kept mum: 'Oh, they're filming *Drag Race* in New Zealand? That'll be amazing! I can't wait to see it!'

* * *

As soon as I heard about the show, I knew that Aussie drag queens Art Simone and Karen from Finance were most likely going to be competing. They both had such strong reputations, I was sure the title would be theirs to lose. Given there would be more Australians watching the show, I knew it would be harder for Kiwi queens to gain the fan support we needed to cross the finish line.

When I entered, I had the mindset that I'd probably be the New Zealander who stayed the longest. I know that probably seems a bit weird, given how terrified I was of going home first – and while talking to my mum had helped a lot, that niggling fear of screwing up royally in episode one was still there. Even so, as cocky as it sounds, I did feel like I was the strongest of the three Kiwi queens. I knew I had great looks and the quick wit needed for the comedy challenges, and I believed in my skill as a lip-syncer and dancer. I thought they would probably want at least one Kiwi to make the final, so I figured that might help me to stick around, but never in a million years did I think that I would win. The title was definitely going to one of those rich Aussie bitches.

Once I was there, all that thinking changed and not in a positive way. Mentally, I was all over the place. All the confidence I'd cultivated going into the show disappeared immediately, and suddenly I felt like I was for sure going to be the first Kiwi sent home. As soon as I checked into the hotel the day before shooting started, I felt like I'd left my self-belief at home.

To make it fair on everyone, no matter where they travelled from, all the queens had to bring the same amount of luggage, and our bags were weighed on arrival by members of the production team. This meant that the three of us who were based in Auckland couldn't just zip home to grab extra pieces. We were also asked if we had any contraband like laptops or phones.

These rules seemed extremely strict, and we were told that crew members would soon be coming to our rooms and searching our bags to make sure we didn't have anything with which we could contact the outside world.

They must have run out of time, because later they told us that our gear wouldn't be searched, but if they found out we had anything on us, we would be removed from the competition immediately. Luckily, I'm long past my bad-boy days, and my phone and laptop were zipped up safely, not to be seen for the entire four-week shoot.

The first night in the hotel was especially weird. The production team didn't want us to know who our competition was, so we were put in our rooms and told not to leave, and minders were stationed in the hallway to make sure we didn't. We were each given a bag with cereal, milk, chips and chocolate in it to see us through to the next day.

If we needed to go out for any reason, we had to knock on our door and then one of the minders would come and see if we had a good enough reason to leave the room. Basically, unless there was a fire, we were staying put.

The first shoot day, I was ready and waiting – in full drag – in my room at 7 am. We'd been told the crew would be coming to get us sometime between 7 and 9 am, so I woke up at 4.30 am, got into my outlandish candy-coloured, foam-wigged, anime cartoon fantasy, then sat there waiting. As I waited, all I could think was 'Holy shit, this is the day that I go on *RuPaul's Drag Race*!' It was completely surreal. I felt like I was about to go skydiving, but I couldn't see how high up the plane was to work out when I'd be jumping out of it.

The first entrance look each queen wears on the show is really important. Even though it isn't officially judged, it's the first thing the show's fans see of you – and, quite often, the fanbase are harsher judges than the ones on the show.

For my first look, I wanted to honour the ultra-camp style of drag that had first captured me and made me want to be a part of this world. When I first started doing drag I almost never wore wigs, but as the years progressed, I started to move with the times and use more fashionable, glamourous looks and real-hair wigs. I didn't want to do that for my entrance look, though. I wanted my fashion on the show to match my journey through drag, so I went hard with the type of drag aesthetic that had first appealed to me. That's why I chose that cartoon look, and to this day I just absolutely love it with its big sleeves, bold colours, cartoonish make-up and massive foam hair.

For this look, I worked with incredible local designer Jen Jones, who also made the 'Bogan Prom Realness' and 'No

Place Like Home' looks I wore in the show. She knew exactly the kind of bright explosion of colour I wanted.

Philmah Bocks, who is the best in the biz, made my hairpiece. I loved it so much that I wore it for a whole lot of promotional appearances for the show. When I appeared on breakfast television, I knew that a lot of viewers would be seeing me for the first time, so I wanted them to see me in my most iconic Kita look. I knew that if they saw me in that look doing a TV interview, then in the show's promotional material and at the start of the episode, there was no way they could forget who I was.

Despite how much I love that look and feel incredible wearing it, I wasn't feeling incredible the morning of the first shoot.

I had planned to take some yellow, pink, green and blue helium balloons, which matched the outfit perfectly. I thought they'd complete the childlike image I wanted to convey, but I wasn't sure if they added to or detracted from what I was doing. The more I stared at them, the more I wondered if they were a bit much. I had quite a bit of time to think about it too.

Even though I was ready, the production team didn't arrive at 7 am. They didn't arrive at 8 am. As time ticked by, I started feeling sillier and sillier as I sat on my hotel bed wearing my foam wig. Eventually, they arrived around 8.30 am.

A young production runner arrived to escort me out of the hotel. Before we left my room, she said very sternly, 'Don't say anything!' I guess they were concerned that if the queens who were still waiting in their rooms heard my voice, they'd be able to work out who else was in the show.

I was herded out of the hotel, into the way-too-bright light of early morning Auckland city. I soon found myself in a van being driven to the studio where my life would change forever. It was only a ten-minute drive from the hotel to the studio, but it was probably the most intense car ride of my life. That's really saying something given my bogan roots and plethora of driving offences!

When we got to the studio, I was hustled inside by a couple of production people. As I walked, a sound guy hurriedly put a mic on me. When we got to a doorway, I was told, 'Walk in there, stand on the mark and say your tagline.'

In mere moments, I'd gone from sitting in a van to being in front of the cameras giving full Kita at 8.45 am.

Just like the first entrance look, a queen's tagline is also really important. This one little line tells the audience who you are and helps cement your brand. I had settled on my tagline just a few days before filming started. Originally, I was just going to say, 'Camp!', but when I was practising it, it just didn't sound quite right. I tried a few different versions, but when I came up with 'How delightfully camp!', it made so much sense – just like Kita Mean, it was cute and silly.

I don't think I gave my tagline the justice it deserved, though, and watching my entrance back makes me cringe a little. I was so blindsided by how quickly we were thrown into the spotlight that I felt completely unprepared. It seemed like I wasn't projecting my voice properly and I was worried I was coming across as timid, rather than my usual effervescent self. Of course, no one else seems to have noticed any of this – I suppose it helps to have an inch of makeup disguising what's really going on underneath the surface!

They were running a very tight operation, so each queen's entrance played out pretty much as quickly as you see them on television. Somehow, though, the crew had managed to get us all into and out of those vans without any of us seeing each other.

Not that it made a difference: I pretty much knew the entire cast before I got on the show. You get told in advance how many costumes you need to make, so you can calculate the number of queens based on that, and then the grapevine does the rest. Between my wigmakers and my dressmakers and the girls around town, nothing's secret!

After each entrance, the next queen was there ready and waiting. It was so quick that when Karen entered the room, she completely missed her mark and just kept walking. I can understand how that happened, as none of us knew we would be jumping straight in like that. I thought for sure there would be some kind of green room, where we'd be given a bit of a briefing about what was going to happen. Nope, recording started immediately. Given the intensity that was running through each of us on that first day, throwing us straight in at the deep end was a good way of immediately bringing the drama out of us.

* * *

The first episode was a trip as we got put through our paces right away. On each episode, we competed in a mini challenge, a maxi challenge and then on the runway. After all of that, RuPaul consulted with the judges to decide the two lowest-scoring queens for the week. Those two queens then got to lip-sync for their lives, with the winner hearing the magic words, 'Shantay, you stay,' and the losing queen being told to 'Sashay away'.

For *Drag Race Down Under*, the judging panel consisted of RuPaul and Michelle Visage along with Aussie comedian Rhys Nicholson. They were joined each week by a celebrity guest judge, either over Zoom or in person.

For the first mini challenge, we performed a fast, furious acting challenge, with Kiwi film director Taika Waititi as a celebrity guest judge. He wasn't able to be there in person, and he may or may not have actually seen what we did, but he definitely looked like he was providing some real-time feedback on the video screen! Because international travel was so difficult, there were a few times in our Covid-riddled season when it might have looked like we were in conversation with someone, but actually we were watching a pre-recorded video. Clever editing, you gotta love it. It was certainly an honour to appear alongside such a legendary Kiwi actor and director, even if we didn't necessarily interact.

For the first week's maxi challenge, which effectively served as the runway as well, we had to serve two separate looks that showcased who we were as queens in a 'Get to Know You' ball.

The first category was 'Born Naked', in which we had to present a nude look, and it felt to me like the people behind the scenes thought this would be an ideal way to get Kita to talk about her big old weight journey.

In every werk room scene, one of the queens asks a question they've clearly been prompted to ask. Luckily for me, it was my sister Elektra who came and asked how I was feeling about doing a nude look, given my weight loss had been so recent. I knew what the producers wanted and I was happy to share my journey.

At that point, I'd been doing drag for ten years, and for nine of those years I had been overweight. I'd learnt to work with my body, and even though my body had been through a big change, I still knew how to make the most of what I had. I have always been confident on stage, no matter how weird or risqué the outfit. To me, the nude challenge was just another opportunity to create a fun look. Besides which, I wasn't even really nude at all. Instead of getting the tears going for me, the challenge meant I just got to make a gorgeous gown in a nude colour, which I looked bloody great in and was a lot of fun to wear.

The second category was 'No Place Like Home', in which we had to do a look inspired by our hometown.

For the show overall, I wanted to flip everything on its head, but for this look, even though it was a bit obvious, I was happy to pick the most clearly iconic Kiwi thing. It just felt right to take the uniform of our most masculine Kiwi icon, our national men's rugby team, the All Blacks, and turn it into a chic drag look. Pretty much every New Zealander, no matter how rarely they watch sport, is patriotic about the All Blacks. The team is known all around the world and even I, a gay man who can't catch a ball, am always proud of them.

Jen Jones worked with me on this one as well, and she was desperate for me to really drag it up. She wanted more embellishments, more sparkles, more fabulousness. But that wasn't what I wanted. I wanted the classic black jersey with a white collar, just like the rugby boys wear. Go the bloody boys! (Was that convincing? It's the first time I've ever said it.)

I thought making the collar and the cuffs a bit larger than life dragged the outfit up enough, and, by keeping the jersey fabric, I was still honouring my inspiration. It's still one of my favourite looks from the show.

Walking the runway in my All Blacks-inspired look, I felt mature and respectful. Standing there like the queen of the country, I felt like I was truly representing and honouring Aotearoa on *Drag Race*.

I wanted to have a rugby ball as part of the look, but it was quite a journey to get the right thing for the show. You might think I'd know exactly what to do with balls, but this one took a while to sort out. Initially, I thought about having a rugby ball as some kind of handbag or clutch, but that was too hard. Then I ordered one that turned out to be a soft toy. It was way too plush and made the whole look seem silly. Then I ordered the real thing, a legit All Blacks branded ball. They make rugby balls in different sizes, like a 4 or a 7. I had no idea what any of it meant so I just picked one at random. It arrived flat, so I had to borrow my nephew's ball pump to inflate it. Once it was pumped up, I rhinestoned it and dragged it up a bit, ready for the show.

Just before I went out on the runway, I was told I couldn't take the ball with me because it had the All Blacks' silver fern on it. The fern is a trademarked logo, which is why the one on my gown was a different shape, but I hadn't thought about the one on the ball.

I quickly decided that there was no way I was heading out there without it, so I took some black gaffer tape from a crew member, slapped it over the fern (completely disrespectful, but going out there without a rugger ball would have been worse) and headed out to the runway. It was the first of many last-minute crafty choices that helped me on my path towards the crown.

My plan was to hold the ball like I was playing and then charge forward as if I was an actual All Black. I also wanted to pass it to the judges, but I thought that might be a bit risky – both because of my ability (or lack thereof) to throw a ball and also because of how Michelle Visage or Ru might react if a queen chucked a ball at their face on day one. I was sure Rhys would love it as I've heard he's a huge fan of balls to the face.

Instead of those sporty moves I tried to hold the rhinestoned ball over my head like a mirror ball then danced beneath it. I don't know if my vision translated through the TV screen, but I felt fabulous doing it.

I was safe for this episode, and while it would have been nice to be in the top, I was relieved that my worst fear of going home first wouldn't be realised.

* * *

I am such a future-focused person that it is hard for me to spend too much time dwelling on the past, which is probably what stopped me from really going deep into my weight journey on the show. I do sometimes think about what my journey would have been if *Drag Race* had come around a few years earlier, back before my surgery.

My brain is so set on moving on that it's hard for me to even remember what life was like before I lost the weight. I imagine that, if I had been the bigger version of myself, my size would have become a huge part (no pun intended) of my place on the show. Every single day I was there, it would have been, 'Whoa, here comes the big momma!' Every single read from the other queens would have been about my weight. Every time we did a dance challenge or anything that involved moving I would have been judged to a different standard. Obviously, some of my costuming would have had to be different. But I don't know that I would have done worse on the show. Maybe my weight would have worked in my favour. Maybe it would have helped me to stand out, making my win even more of a sure thing. The truth is I always saw my size as a big advantage to me as a drag performer.

Drag is about spectacle, and when I was at my biggest, I truly was a spectacle. My size paired with my outrageous make-up, huge looks and larger-than-life performances really meant all eyes were on me. What helped was that I didn't even think of myself as big. I'd always been so lost in my own thoughts that I would barely be thinking about it. Then I might walk past a shop window, catch sight of myself and think, 'God, she's a big bitch!' But as soon as the window was out of my eyeline, I would forget again. At least, I would forget until I sprained my ankle for the millionth time while dancing in heels, something that happened about once a month back then (eventually a diagnosis of gout explained it). In my mind, I was this extreme glam goddess, and to the people who saw me, I was this beast of a thing with the confidence of a glam goddess. It was a great combination for a performer.

Growing up the size I did also helped me develop my sense of humour. When you're big and you don't want people to talk about you, you quickly learn to be the first one to make a joke about your weight, and that always has to be a better joke than anyone else could come up with. That kind of thinking led me to be the quick-witted MC I am today.

For an audience, I think it also makes me a bit more relatable. If I was this unattainable beauty, that would be intimidating, and my jokes wouldn't pop like they do. It was always such a thrill to be in front of an audience, with a body type that so many would see as a flaw, but completely owning it – I think crowds loved that. In these ways, my weight was an advantage as I built my career. I grew up big, and being big helped me develop the humour and confidence that is so key to being Kita.

By the time I was on the show, I had all that personality *and* I could fit into some fabulous gowns. Maybe because I didn't have any distractions during filming, I had the opportunity to work through some of these thoughts, but for now, I had to get on with the task at hand – kicking butt no matter what.

* * *

At the end of the first episode, my sister Elektra and Aussie Indigenous queen Jojo Zaho lip-synced for their lives to 'Tragedy' by the Bee Gees. While I was sad to see Elektra in the bottom, I wasn't surprised. I agreed with the judges that her looks hadn't quite stacked up against the others. Still, I was absolutely rooting for her to make it through the lip-sync, and was super chuffed when her incredible performance saved her from elimination.

Jojo went home despite making a sickening impression and earning scores of fans. Almost immediately, people were calling out for her return. A lot of people want her back on another season and I agree, her brand of Faboriginal drag is extraordinary and she has so much more to show.

After shooting the first episode, we had an unexpected few days off. Given we had time to kill, production did something I never thought they would do: they let us out. We were able to break into small groups and head out into the city. Karen from Finance, Etcetera Etcetera and I went out to a gorgeous Auckland beach called Mission Bay, where we ate at a German cafe looking out at the water. We even drank a little bit of wine even though we were on strict no-booze instructions.

It was a nice chance to relax because from then on, it was all go. It was up early, shoot 'til late at night, get home, practise the next lip-sync song, stone a costume or rehearse your choreography, then go to bed for a few hours before it all started again.

CHAPTER 11

Start your engines

WHEN IT COMES TO *Drag Race Down Under*, there is one episode that everyone always asks about: the 'Snatch Game' episode. During this celebrity impersonation challenge, each queen takes on the role of a different famous person, then takes part in a fast-paced game show. It was a wild episode.

While some have called it the worst Snatch Game ever across all of the show's franchises, it did showcase one of the best performances ever seen on the show. To top all that off, it also featured what was easily the most dramatic and controversial elimination of the season. While there was a lot going on for viewers, there was even more going on behind the scenes.

Originally, I thought about doing the legendary drag queen Divine as my character because I knew I could definitely pull off her look. The problem was I couldn't work out how to make her funny and, even worse, I couldn't really do her voice. Divine's voice is so husky and gritty that it somehow sounds both high and low at the same time. The more I tried, the worse it got. I needed some better options, so before shooting started, I went to talk to my sister.

Anita had already locked in doing Queen Elizabeth II from the get-go, and it was such a good pick. It's a character everyone knows and she's someone who has plenty to talk about. Anita also had a spot-on look and a great voice to go with it. I was jealous – she had a perfect choice already figured out, and she even had a few solid back-up characters ready to go. Meanwhile, I was really unsure about who to do.

When I asked Anita for help, she had some great ideas for me too. One of them was Ozzy Osbourne, which could have been really funny. Eventually, after brainstorming with her, I settled on Carole Baskin from *Tiger King*. She was an extremely topical icon, who was on everyone's mind at the time as everyone seemed to have been watching that show during lockdown.

Carole had a fun look to pull from and I had some great gags prepared: 'I'm pretty sure my husband ran off with a homosexual because everyone online said I drove him to the Grindr.'

I could have killed it with Carole – but Anita had one more suggestion. 'You're so good at creating rhymes off the top of your head. You're constantly doing little jingles and making stuff rhyme. You should just do Dr Seuss.'

I thought it was a really clever idea and, if I pulled it off, it would have been a fabulous showcase of my talents. I took both looks to the show with me and kept thinking about it. I was sure I could pull off both, but I didn't feel like either of them would be a winning Snatch Game performance. Right up until the day of filming I hadn't decided which one I'd do, so I pulled over my support network – Anita and Elektra – to see what they thought. Anita encouraged me to do Dr Seuss, 'if that's what you feel most comfortable with'. This was the challenge that scared me the most, so I decided to face that fear head on by making the riskier choice.

Little did I know what Miss Wigl'it was really thinking behind that sweet smile of hers … In the episode, just before she encourages me to do Dr Seuss, we see her in a confessional saying, 'I would *never* sabotage anyone!', before winking at the camera. I don't know if she was genuinely trying to sabotage me in that moment, or if she just thought saying that would make good television!

The whole Snatch Game experience was surreal and a little overwhelming. There I was on the same set on which I'd seen so many people I idolise absolutely kill it. The stools we had to sit on were pretty shit, so that was a bit of a boner killer, but besides that, everything was just how I thought it would be.

I walked onto the set thinking, 'This is it! Here I am, about to be part of *Drag Race* herstory.' I just didn't know if it was going to be for the right reasons or the wrong ones.

I had been practising my improvisation skills, getting my sisters to throw me words and, within seconds, I would come up with a perfect rhyming answer. So it could have been a successful Snatch Game for me, if only I hadn't screwed up my first introduction. Through all my practices, I'd forgotten that I would have to riff with Ru right at the top, and I just was not at all ready for it.

Ru came at me with an easy volley: 'Do you like green eggs and ham?'

My plan had been to think of the final word of my rhyme first, then work back from there to come up with the first half. When done properly, it's a good trick to make yourself look clever, because everyone thinks you're coming up with the perfect rhyme as you're talking.

I crumbled under the pressure and screwed up when Ru asked me about the damn green eggs. I ended my first sentence with the word 'delicious', which I should have been saving for the end of the second line. I scrambled for a moment to come up with a rhyme and, if I'm honest, I have no idea what I said. It's like I blacked out for a second.

I was mortified. I just kept thinking, 'You've absolutely fucked it, girl.'

I knew as soon as it happened, the shade rattle would be sounded after my answer, so I decided to double down on my performance, so they wouldn't have any more chances to make me look bad in the edit. I figured if I just stayed in character, kept my face on and performed whether the cameras were on me or not, I would leave them nothing to use to make me look like I was bombing it. I stayed in it the whole time, so focused, and I didn't let myself mess up any of my other answers in the same way. It was terrifying, but I got through it, and when they called 'Cut!' I was so relieved.

When I look back at my performance as Dr Seuss, all I can say is cringe, cringe, cringe, cringe. I'd been terrified of Snatch Game before, during and after, and I felt my attempt to portray the master of children's rhyme had been a spectacular failure. But after that first fumble, my performance had improved, and I knew I had done all that I could – and maybe, just maybe, I'd done a good enough job to scrape by.

One of the queens – who shall remain nameless – disagreed with me on that, later telling an interviewer that every time I had to give an answer, there was a thirty- or forty-second pause before I thought of what to say. Everyone else who was there will dispute that, but, hey, girl probably wanted to make herself feel better about her own weird, rambling performance.

After we wrapped the shoot that night and on the morning of the elimination, so many of the others, perhaps a bit misguidedly, felt extremely confident about their Snatch Game, but not me. I was at peak anxiety. I felt like I was 100 per cent done for and I was certain I was going to be the first Kiwi sent home.

After the cameras stopped rolling, I confessed these fears to my sister Anita. I don't know if she was trying to keep my expectations low or what, but she said straight to my face, 'Yeah, I think you're probably going to be in the bottom.'

It was ruthless, especially because whenever she felt low during the competition, I would do everything I could to lift her back up. In some ways, I think it might have been easier on us if we had each appeared on different seasons, but I also loved seeing my sister across the (admittedly quite small) werk room.

Once we got to the runway critiques, though, there was a huge mood shift in the other queens, and I absolutely loved it. Earlier that day, as we had been preparing for the runway, Scarlet – who'd done Jennifer Coolidge – and Art – who'd taken on Bindi Iriwn – had been gushing about themselves, saying things like 'I honestly believe that will go down as one of the best Snatch Games in history.'

I was sitting there, doing my make-up, listening to them, feeling terrified and thinking, 'Whoop-de-doo for you two!'

Their high energy started to drive me lower because I was so focused on my own Snatch Game performance and I just wasn't feeling anywhere near as confident as they were. It was such a blur that I instantly thought that they must have been right – they had done amazingly, and I was the only one feeling like shit. So when the tables were turned on them … it was delicious.

It was clear that Anita had left all of us in the dust – the jokes were there, the look was right and Ru lost it at everything she said. No one could have caught her after that performance. But, after all the talk and worry, and with the Sea Sickening runway over and done with, I ended up in what was effectively equal second place along with Etcetera. I wondered if maybe the judges just didn't want to talk about Etcetera's choice of character – Lindy Chamberlain – because honestly, the less said about that the better.

We were named the top three and headed back to the werk room. When the other queens came back and told us that all six of them were up for elimination (instead of the usual two), I tried to keep my cool but inside I was so happy. What a delightfully camp series of events.

Who knows, maybe someone up top had a soft spot for me, which was how I escaped the terrifying bottom six that day.

The good news didn't stop there. When the bottom six was narrowed down to the bottom two, the queen we all considered the biggest threat in the competition, Art Simone, was there lip-syncing for her life against Coco Jumbo. In a dramatic turn of events, Art was the one sent packing – and I was 100 per cent there for it.

* * *

Quirky, kooky, kitsch, quick and keen

Hashtag team Kita Mean

Social clown with a side of vamp

Put my face on a stamp, she's the queen of camp

Live life, laugh to live

If you can't love yourself, what you got to give?

I'm here to boast, I'm the host with the most

So, get engrossed in this overdose!

My lyrics for 'Queens Down Under'

Before going on the show, whenever I watched *Drag Race* at home, the challenge where the girls team up to create their own Spice Girls–style groups and sing original verses was always the one I wanted a chance to do. Getting to be up there with your sisters, living your girl-band fantasy, looked like so much fun. Plus, I knew I was a whizz at writing lyrics, so I figured it would be one challenge I could definitely smash. And I feel like I did!

Episode three's girl-group challenge, in which we got to record vocals and perform together, was one of my favourites (but I wish I'd got more credit for 'Put my face on a stamp, she's the queen of camp!' My lyrics popped off!).

Our song 'Queens Down Under' was so much fun to write and record, and I was so delighted we got to record our vocals with the amazing Michelle Visage.

Then, during my first go at recording, I absolutely stuffed it. Because I tend to write lyrics and rhymes so fast, I hadn't really written mine out properly. They were scribbled in the same chaotic way my brain works, so when I stepped up to the mic to record, they came out just as chaotic and messy.

Michelle kindly let me take a couple of minutes to write them out clearly, then I came back and slayed it. I got it in one take, and she kept gassing me up: 'It's so good, Kita', 'I can't believe you got that so fast, Kita!'

Every time she said my name, it just made me so happy. *The* Michelle Visage! We were done so quickly that she asked, 'Should we record it in French now?'

Having recorded the track, we then had to perform it for the judges. As good as the record was, I felt like my performance wasn't quite as shit hot as I know it could have been. If I had killed it on stage, like I had in the booth, I would have been a real contender for the win. Alas, Scarlet nabbed the first of her three wins. Bitch!

I did get a small win that week, though. At the judgement table, Ru said something that I think confused a lot of viewers, but which I absolutely loved. She said: 'When you get in drag, there's just something that's kind of cross-dresser-y, like when a cross-dresser gets into drag.'

I 100 per cent got it. And I 100 per cent took it as a huge compliment. I knew exactly what she was getting at. I love getting into drag and I feel like there's an energy that comes through me when I'm in drag. I get a kick from putting these ladies' clothes on. I just feel so cool, I love it. I didn't realise this was obvious to anybody else, but I guess there is a glint in my eye that gives it away. Even though what Ru said sounded like a read, I totally agreed with her and I totally loved it.

While episode three was a great episode for me, it was a tough week for my sister Elektra. When we split into two groups, I ended up in one – Three and a Half Men – with Elektra, Karen from Finance and Maxi Shield. Based on the vibe in our team, I really felt like it was going to be Elektra's week as she was born to perform and dance. She led our team with such kindness and softness, showing so much respect for each of the queens in the group, that we just could not stop raving to her about it. She took our four-person group, with a wild assortment of skill levels, and got us to put on what felt like a pretty slick, unified performance. The judges, however, saw things differently.

From our perspective, a win was definitely on the cards for her. When the critiques came, it was hard to watch. We all felt terrible because we had been boosting her up, telling her what a great job she had done. It felt like we had let her down.

Elektra was called a show-off, and it felt like some of what looked like 'showing off' might just have been because Maxi, Karen and I didn't hit the standard we needed to. Elektra had been so conscious of making sure there was room for everyone in the number, and it didn't feel right that she didn't get credit for that. Yeah, she did some high kicks and jumps – because she can! Why wouldn't you?

Elektra had been going through some stuff backstage with some of the girls being really unfriendly to her, so to see her be hit with such harsh critiques was heartbreaking. She had done a great job, so to see her fall to the bottom was devastating.

I was on my own journey that week, having being told that my look for the 'Bogan Prom Realness' runway was not bogan enough, even though I was probably the only true bogan on the stage.

I'd taken the things that said 'bogan' to me when I'd fully embraced that lifestyle as a teenager and paid homage to them. All those Saturday nights in the cemeteries, all those Sunday afternoons drinking 12-per-centers in the garage – they were woven into the fabric of that neon-green dress. I knew I could maybe have done a broader version of a bogan look, inspired by Swanndris, beer cans and Nissan Skylines, but I wanted to do something that said bogan to me, and I wanted to create a look that honoured the bogan I had once been.

The judges couldn't understand it. They didn't get it, and that's fine. I was happy to do a runway that was more for me than them, and since then I've had a lot of messages from people who got it and loved it.

* * *

Our filming days were structured like this: we had about two hours max to shave, dress, and do hair and nails – about one hour less than I normally take. The challenges took place on the first day, then on the morning of the second day, we'd get into our confessional looks and record our pieces to camera about the previous day's shoot. Once the confessionals were done, we'd get into our boy looks and head into the werk room to film the start of the next day, which is where we're getting ready for the runway and typically asking each other invasively personal questions we would normally never ask. We'd then spend the second half of the day filming the runway and the elimination.

There are stories about *Drag Race*, of queens standing there onstage for hours and hours, but from what I can remember the runway and judging didn't take that long. But I was safe a lot – so I could leave the stage! There were moments offstage when we'd be standing around, and maybe someone would be talking to Ru, and I was so conscious of not being in the way that often I would stand there and stare at the floor until someone needed me again. After so long being the bad kid in life, here I was trying desperately to be the good one!

A lot of the international reaction to the show criticised our cast for being too mean to each other, and I think this was partly a result of the fast pace of the shoot. I think this was also because there was a bit of a cultural difference that maybe confused some Americans and Brits. What seemed like us being mean to each other was actually just the way Aussies and Kiwis show love. We constantly roast each other, as that is our way of showing our friendship. Admittedly, though, some of the meanness didn't come from a good place.

For the first few episodes, from my end, the vibes between the cast seemed very friendly. I later heard from Elektra that right from the get-go people were really getting on her, even when the cameras weren't rolling, but I didn't see that. I saw people getting along!

Perhaps I only had this impression because I had no idea what the queens were saying in their confessionals. In my own confessionals, I'd been making flippant jokes, but I hadn't really been calling anyone out. I certainly wasn't saying anything about anyone I wouldn't say in the werk room.

But even after seeing the show, I still don't understand the perception that the *Down Under* queens were bitchier than the girls on other international seasons. Maybe it's our accents that make us sound mean? Whatever the cause, when I watch the season back, it still feels like we were all just having fun – because we were!

CHAPTER 12

Struggle bug

THE FASHION SENSE OF drag queens has evolved to the point where *Drag Race* girls are both inspiring international fashion week runways and even walking on the runways themselves. As that has happened it's got harder and harder to get by with some shabby sewing skills and a hot-glue gun when it comes to the sewing challenge. Showing whether we can make outfits all on our own in the space of just a few hours really separates the women from the girls.

Episode four was sewing challenge week for us. I knew it was going to be a tough week, but I had no idea just how tough. Our challenge was all about taking some trash and turning it into a runway-ready outfit, a true classic.

The pile of trash in the werk room had a certain surprise in it, though – a surprise that would have us gagged and throw a real spanner in the works when it came to my journey to the crown.

Hidden in that pile of garbage was Art Simone – and it looked good on her! By the time we got there, that wagon full of junk she was hiding in had been there for a while. Poor old Art must have got a sore back lying in there for so long.

The surprise on our faces when she jumped out was genuine. Quite how the crew managed to sneak the loudest queen out of Melbourne into the werk room without any of us knowing, I have no idea. To be honest with you, I felt like an audience member watching the show at that point. I was excited by this new and unexpected twist. I felt almost like a giddy kid doing a live action role play of *Drag Race*. It didn't feel real; it was as though I was imagining the gag that was unfolding in front of me.

A lot of viewers were confused about Art's return to the competition. There didn't seem to be any rhyme or reason to why it happened – she was just back. Plenty of people were upset that Coco and Jojo weren't given any kind of chance to fight their way back in. Instead, it was given to Art and announced almost like it was nothing.

Whatever the reason for Art's return, it worked out for all of us because we got to enjoy all of the amazing runways she brought.

* * *

Even though I probably should have been intimidated by one of the toughest competitors arriving back in the ring, I just thought it was camp and fun and a good gag.

Maybe I was deluded, and that delusion might have continued into that week's maxi challenge. I thought my look, which was made out of blue sleeping bag material with elastic cable ties to attach balls from an actual ball-pit and bra covers made from an umbrella, was very me – fun, camp and attention-grabbing in all the right ways. My competitors did not share my opinion.

None of this footage ended up being aired, but I remember all the other queens were mocking it and laughing at it. They called it an eyesore, and said it was ugly, hideous and every other synonym there was for 'bad to look at'. I did not get one single compliment from any of the other girls. It was a rough day for me.

The others' comments had got to me to the point where I was sure I'd be one of the bottom queens that week. I said to Anita, 'Girl, what do you think? I like it.'

She replied, 'Yeah, I think the others are right. You might be in trouble.'

My best friend wasn't even coming through with the support I needed. That was hard, especially as I'd been giving her as much support as I could. If I'm honest, I didn't think her book and VHS tape dress was great, but there wasn't anything to be gained by me adding extra criticism, so I told her she would be fine and that her outfit wasn't that bad.

I even went out of my way to help her. The skirt she had made wasn't fitting right, so I shifted it and resewed it while she was wearing it, and all the while I was building her back up, telling her she was going to be okay – and all of that time I could have been working on my own outfit.

I'd originally planned to have balls shooting out of the dress to make it really pop, but because of the time constraints, I couldn't make it happen. Well, it was partly because of the time constraints and partly because I didn't have the skills!

Even though the other queens' opinions made me feel shitty about my outfit, I still feel proud of what I did; I think I looked bright, fun and very Kita – and I had a ball (ha ha) wearing it. And if I did have to lip-sync, I was so fucking ready.

After the sewing challenge, having had every other queen tell me how shitty my ball dress looked, I went back to the hotel and got to work. I'd smuggled some things off set. In fact, I was constantly smuggling things off set. Every day, I'd take a can of hairspray home with me, and I'd always take snacks too. If one of the other queens wanted a can of Red Bull, they knew there'd be some in my hotel-room fridge as I took as many cans as I could carry home with me every day. Everyone knew about it, so my nickname on set became Klepto Kita.

On this day, I took some marker pens, extra balls and some socks. Using them, I made some absolutely glorious sock puppets, and I had a great plan for them. That week's lip-sync song was 'I Begin to Wonder' by Dannii Minogue, and there's a bit in the chorus where some backing vocalists do some extra lines, which come in fast. My plan was to have the sock puppets hidden in my dress, then I would pull them out to lip-sync to the backing vocals. It would have been a gag, but, unfortunately, I did too well to have to bring the puppets out. Poor me!

Going into the show with Anita, I was sure that we would be played off against each other. If I'd been producing, I would have made it happen – what a great storyline! This episode, when we were both terrified about our looks, seemed like the perfect opportunity to have that happen – but it didn't. To this day, I'm still surprised they didn't put us in the bottom two and make us lip-sync against each other. It would have been great TV. (And I could have smashed her …)

Unfortunately, Karen's Schapelle Corby–inspired outfit, which had involved almost no sewing, was just so bad that they couldn't put me in the bottom two. Karen and Anita ended up battling, and Wiggles was the one who got sent home.

In the footage that aired, you don't see this, but when she got called into the bottom two, I was a mess straight away. I was really trying to hold it together, but it was not happening. I didn't want anyone to see that I was upset, and I definitely didn't want to try and take focus away from Anita and Karen. I was just standing there trying not to do anything, with tears rolling down my face. Between takes I had my head down and when they called action, I had to pull my head up, but as soon as there was a cut I went straight back to staring at the floor.

I knew how much it meant to her. I knew how much she wanted to prove herself. It was pretty brutal that, after trouncing everyone in Snatch Game, Anita was sent home the same week that the person who had bombed the hardest at it came back.

I admit I was a little surprised at just how emotional I got when Anita was eliminated. I knew I would be upset about seeing my friend go, but I had no idea how hard it would hit me. She is my best friend, my rock and the person I have spent more time with than anyone else in the world over the past few years. That said, I think some part of how I felt was a bit of a release, as our relationship during filming had started to strain in ways I hadn't expected.

* * *

Anita and I have always made jokes about the hierarchy of our relationship, right down to the fact that my name comes before hers when people refer to us. We are officially Kita and Anita, and that's the way it goes.

When those types of jokes get repeated over and over –
and I'm guilty of it; when we entered the werk room for the
first time, I made a little dig about Anita riding my coattails –
they start to create a bit of insecurity.

Like me, I think Anita wanted to use this show as an
opportunity to prove herself as a solo performer. I think she
hates being seen as my sidekick, just like I hate only being
seen as part of a duo. People have called her the Robin to my
Batman, and I know those comparisons grate on her.

We respect each other, but I think we each believe we're a
better queen than the other. Almost every queen who enters
Drag Race must think she is the best one there, and having
that kind of self-confidence is helpful, but it also adds an extra
layer of weirdness when you usually work as a twosome.

Even though we both knew that reality television is
structured to create a story, and our placings in the show
weren't the one and only defining way to tell who the superior
queen was, we both wanted to be the queen who got further
than the other. Then, when it happened, it didn't feel good
at all.

For whatever reason, from the moment we entered the
werk room, Anita decided to put some distance between us.
She immediately set up in a different part of the room and,
while Elektra and I were constantly in our corner together,
Anita was usually off hanging out with Art and some of the
other Aussie queens. She didn't speak to me often and when

she did it was rarely supportive. I tried to pull her over to have a bit of fun, but she just wasn't game.

I thought it would be helpful for both of us to push our duo during the show, but she obviously didn't see it that way. It was strange because the producers didn't really try to pit us against each other in the way we thought they might, but somehow there ended up being a block put between us anyway. It wasn't picked up by the cameras, so I don't know what was going on or why it was happening.

The invisible wall that Anita seemed to put up frustrated me and made me feel a bit of resentment. I understood that she wanted to prove herself, but I felt hurt. It sometimes seemed as though she didn't value what I was bringing, because she is such a head-girl-style professional – always on time, always organised, always ready for any gig. I'm a bit more of a mess, more rambunctious, so I sometimes feel like she looks down on me. Even so, I give a lot to what the two of us have – in energy, in creativity, in being game for anything. I always hustle for Anita to be a part of anything I do. Any gig I get, I try to hook my girl up too.

While we filmed *Drag Race*, I started to feel like she thought she would be better off without me, or like I was in her way. It was hard because I felt like the opposite was closer to the truth.

Beating Anita did not feel good at all. When it happened, all I felt was devastation. It wasn't devastation that she was gone – I just felt super, super shitty for her, so that's where all the emotion came from.

When the whole season wrapped, things didn't go back to how they'd been before filming. When I got home after the shoot and we got back to work, I did some things that made the situation worse.

Given how long I was away, it would have been clear that I'd made it right through to the final and that I had a shot at winning. When I walked into Caluzzi for our first rehearsal after the show, I did a full clowning routine, miming a huge crown, pretending to buckle under its weight and not knowing where to put it. I thought I was being hilarious. I wasn't.

A few days later, Anita messaged me to call me out. She said, 'To be honest, girl, I feel like there's zero respect for me, like you have no respect about how I feel about the situation, and like you're just trying to rub it in my face that you got to the end.'

She was right – not about me trying to rub it in her face, but about me not being at all sensitive to the situation.

Being on the show, given its position in drag culture, feels like the be all and end all. It feels like what happens on the show will stick on you for the rest of your career, that it's all you will be known for. That's not true, though. It's not everything – but it is massive. It has changed both of our lives.

Reality television is a strange world and when you're there, making it, it's almost impossible to be the true version of yourself. What people see is the version of me who behaved differently when the cameras were on me, the version of me who was obsessed with the competition. Real life isn't a competition where people are eliminated, though. Real life is work and fun and everything in between.

The rift between me and Anita is an odd thing to talk about because, from the outside, it looked like things couldn't have gone better for us. People were so gutted when Anita left, saying it was clearly not her time, and the fan support for her was huge.

At the end of the season, the contestants all vote on who should be named Miss Congeniality. Anita was the obvious and deserved winner of the title. She left a massive mark with her legendary Snatch Game, she had all the judges obsessed with her manic smile, and she served adorable talking heads in the confessional. She will definitely be back on the show again in some way, I just know it.

The two of us came out of the show with so much love and fan support, and we are so lucky for that. Things were weird between us for a while, but they are better now. We're back to being besties. There's no hard feelings. Thankfully, anything that happened on the show is in the past, and now we continue to work together, and continue to kill at everything we do.

* * *

It was a pity Anita didn't stick around so I could do the brutal read I had planned for her. Episode five started with the reading challenge, where we each take turns making the most cutting jokes we can about each other, and I had some doozies for my sister: 'You're so boring and white, I was going to make a racist joke and then I realised you are one!'

Everyone was sure I was going to win the reading challenge and, overall, I felt like I killed it the best, but Art had two amazing reads on Elektra and Etcetera, which were such hits with Ru that Art took the win.

I will forever be proud that I wrote all of my reads myself. I had no idea that getting other people to help write your jokes was even something anyone on *Drag Race* could do, and apparently I was in the minority on that.

After filming each day, we'd all be driven home in a couple of vans. One day, the other girls just started chatting about the reading challenge. They talked about how they'd hired comedians to write reads for them, how they'd worked with writers to prepare jokes for Snatch Game and how they'd worked on their lyrics for *Drag Race* with songwriters.

Of course, this all had to have happened before the show as, once we were in, we didn't have phones or laptops so we couldn't get any outside help. Even so, this was all still a massive surprise to me.

For one thing, it means they were writing their reads before they actually knew who their competitors were, so they probably had to rethink some of the gags they'd prepared once they met the other dolls. Similarly, their lyrics would have been written blind, and they probably had to rewrite them once they heard the actual track they would be singing to. Still, my mind was blown. It had never occurred to me to get help with preparing jokes and lyrics.

They all talked about it so nonchalantly, as if it was just the done thing, and I was sitting there so naive to the fact that this might ever happen.

It makes sense, though; we walk down the runways in looks we haven't sewn ourselves, so of course people get help with the other parts of the show. Even so, it was pretty astonishing and it really underlined the disparity of resources between us.

Some of the other girls posted videos of them getting ready, and they're in a room with ten other people all rhinestoning a gown together. I would never post videos of me getting ready, because it would literally just be a clip of me eating KFC on the floor while I bedazzle my looks as Trinity Ice watches on from the couch, laughing.

If I did it all again, though, I wouldn't change a thing. I wouldn't want my lounge packed out with people helping me finish my clothes. I wouldn't want to be doing jokes and singing lyrics written by other people. I have no judgement for the queens who did get a bit of help, but it certainly makes me very proud that I was able to take the crown while using the words that came out of my own manic, cross-dresser-y brain.

* * *

The reading challenge led us into what must be one of the most vulgar maxi challenges of all time. In the marketing challenge, we all had to write and act in our own ad for a unique brand of yeast spread that we'd created – and every queen went out there and did something absolutely disgusting. Come on, though, it was yeast spread – they knew exactly where all of our minds were going to go.

There is an unfortunate trend among some drag artists to make fun of women and female bodies, and I believe that type of humour is the exact opposite of what drag is all about. Drag performance is a space to subvert gender expectations, not to reinforce tired and misogynistic ideas that have been perpetrated by men for years.

Now, I'm not saying that what I came up with was some kind of lofty high art – very quickly, I thought of Yeasty Nuts, a doughnut filling for your ring. Looking back, I could have spent some more time on it, but, even though my jokes were gross, they were not degrading to women. I didn't create an all-time hilarious ad, but watching it back, I don't feel any shame.

I'd wanted to honour the legendary drag queen Divine's iconic dog-poo eating scene in *Pink Flamingos*, so I put on my unused Snatch Game look and did my own version of it, spreading the disgusting, off-brand spread all over my face and round my nose. Even though – like most Kiwis – I enjoy the flavour of our national yeast spread more than overseas tourists do, it was still too much. I was gagging from it. Then someone told me, a little too late, that RuPaul does not like watching people eat.

I saw Elektra when I left the set, and she had also been putting it in her mouth and up her nose, and I thought to myself, 'Oh, no, we're done for.'

My 'Finest Sheila in the Bush' runway was one of the most beautiful pieces I brought, although I'm not sure it looked as fantastic on camera as I had hoped it would. I knew people were going to go more for a bush-woman, going harder with the more rugged ideas that the theme gave them. Instead, I wanted to take something beautiful from the bush. I decided to be surrounded by flying butterflies. It was an ambitious idea, and one that I was sure would turn heads and get people excited.

Butterflies have been part of some disasters on previous *Drag Race* seasons, but I was sure that wouldn't be the case this time. My face was supposed to be surrounded by these butterflies, which had rubber-band wings that I could wind up and propellers that made them flutter around. Unfortunately, if you didn't know they were there, you'd miss them – and even if you did know they were there, you still might not be able to see them.

Luckily, because my eating scene in the marketing challenge had been a reference and one that I knew Ru would love, I ended up being safe. And Elektra? Well, she snagged her first win. I was so proud of my girl.

It didn't really matter how the ads or the butterflies went, though, because that episode will always be remembered not for any of the costumes on display or any of the yeast spread gross-outs, but for RuPaul calling out Scarlet Adams' earlier use of blackface in her live shows. It was one of the most shocking moments on the show. The choices Scarlet had made were unacceptable, and to see Ru call them out was incredibly intense.

It turned out that Scarlet had brought it up in the werk room. Etcetera's response to Scarlet's revelation was measured, clear and concise, and she didn't offer any opportunity to let Scarlet's actions be excused.

I'm not sure who else had heard that conversation, but the first *I* heard of it was when Ru started talking about it on the runway – and even then, I didn't really hear the whole thing as I was tied so incredibly tightly into my corset that I was essentially going in and out of consciousness as we were receiving our critiques. I was lucky I didn't faint.

When Ru gave Scarlet the opportunity to address her prior use of blackface, to her credit, Scarlet immediately owned up to it, saying she had made mistakes that she regretted every day.

'I regret the fact that I used my platform as a performer to ridicule people who've faced systematic racism for hundreds of years, and I'm so ashamed of the person that I once was. I'm really sorry to you and to everyone that I have hurt.'

Ru responded that she wanted this to be a lesson in humility and accountability, and that she hoped Scarlet would learn and grow from her mistakes.

When Ru finished addressing Scarlet, we all went back out to the werk room while the judges deliberated. As soon as I walked offstage, I immediately took my costume off and threw it across the room. The production assistants were so confused. Eventually, they worked out that I needed help to get untied from the corset. I was in so much pain that I could barely concentrate on what was going on.

Maxi Shield and Etcetera Etcetera ended up in the bottom two, with both queens giving a very entertaining lip-sync performance to the classic banger 'Absolutely Everybody' by Vanessa Amorosi. It was a close contest, but in the end Etcetera sashayed away.

* * *

In the thick of the makeover challenge in episode six, I was in the worst mental state that I'd been in during the entire show. I thought for sure I would be going home. Everything was amplified by the fact that I wasn't really sleeping. We were shooting till late into the night, then eating late and only having so many hours to shower, learn the lip-sync for the next day and sleep before doing it all over again.

It was the worst anxiety ever. I'd compounded so much pressure inside myself to be better than my best, and internally I was beating myself up for not being as good as I could be. When I'm in that spiral, I can't get out of it. I was convinced I was a loser, and it was affecting my work. So it might surprise you to find out that I hit my lowest low on the week that we got to hang out with hot gay rugby players and put them into drag.

I have a love–hate relationship with doing other people's make-up. I hate the process, but I love the finished product. I'm the same about exercising.

During the 'Drag Family Resemblance' challenge, which involved making over a rugby player so that we looked like we were related, I got to make over Karl, an absolutely stunning member of the Falcons, an Auckland gay rugby team. Karl's partner, Brad, was also in the werk room, being made over by Scarlet.

As every queen had a rugby player to make over, there were twice as many people in the werk room as usual. This meant there was much less space for lighting, cameras and sound to be set up around us, so a lot of our make-up had to be shifted around.

As a result, I ended up painting Karl in a completely different set-up to what I was used to, and then I got moved to another new place partway through the challenge. Meanwhile, Karl was going through a unique experience with the love of his life, and they were busy talking about what was happening. To top it all off, Karl had never had someone do his face before so he couldn't sit still. To make good TV, they needed him to tell some of his story, but it would have been great if he could have told it while I wasn't trying to concentrate on doing his face!

In the end, I didn't feel like I'd even been close to getting it right. In fact, I felt like he looked like trash. I felt like I'd made him look like some kind of demented clown, but he seemed happy, and when he saw himself, he immediately called out, 'Yeah! Camp!'

When we took lunch, I was truly shitting bricks – and no one wants to be shitting while they're eating. After lunch, I had an hour and a half before the challenge to whack on my face, so I headed to my station to get to work.

I moved all of my make-up back to my mirror where it belonged, but something was missing. There was a specific gel eyeliner that I needed. It was fundamental to how I wanted to do my face. I couldn't find it anywhere, so I started freaking out.

I walked around, snapping at anyone that asked what was going on with me. A few of the production assistants offered to help, but I was just not having it. I had a full meltdown, like an absolute divalicious drama queen.

'THERE'S NOTHING THAT CAN BE DONE! I CAN'T FUCKING DO MY MAKE-UP WITHOUT THIS THING! IF I DIDN'T HAVE TO MOVE MY FUCKING SHIT OVER THERE, IT WOULDN'T BE GONE. YOU MADE ME MOVE IT. AND LOOK AT KARL. HIS MAKE-UP LOOKS LIKE SHIT!'

Karen, always one of the kindest people around, said, 'Hey, sis, will this work?'

She offered me an eyeliner that was almost nothing like the one I had, but I decided to forge ahead with it anyway.

Just as I was about to start using it, one of the crew said, 'Oh, is this it?'

It was my gel eyeliner. It had rolled off my desk and under my wardrobe, and had been found barely a metre from my station. I now had what I needed to do my face. But I had just made the most dramatic scene about it. I felt pretty sheepish. I can't think of many times in my professional life when I have behaved like that.

I'd behaved so badly that I decided I had to apologise to the production team. Before I could move on I got everyone's attention.

'Hey, look, I just want to apologise. There's no excuse for me snapping. This is super high stakes, and I was super stressed and I don't like the person that I become when I'm like that. I feel really shitty about it and I'm really sorry.'

Everyone else was at pains to reassure me that it was a non-event, but I still felt deeply embarrassed.

I still didn't feel like I'd done a great job on Karl's make-up either. In fact, I thought it could be time for me to start packing my suitcases.

Once we had our looks on, though, I couldn't believe it. We looked camp, we looked brilliant – and we looked like twins. I know that we looked like twins because a couple of times during the day, people started talking to Karl thinking he was me. The first time it happened, I clicked to the fact that this could actually be my week after all.

In front of the judges, Karl got the opportunity to share the value of manaakitanga, and I'm so happy he got to do it on such a massive stage. Manaakitanga is a Māori concept that describes being generous and respectful of those around you, showing aroha or love, and expressing the way we can lift each other's spirits up. On that day, Karl did that for me, and I am so grateful to have worked with such a compassionate person. His energy was exactly what a high-strung queen at her wits' end needed.

Winning was a complete surprise to me. When we got back into the werk room after the judges' feedback, I was a bit like a stunned mullet.

Karen said to me, 'Why are you so glum? You just won the challenge.'

I explained that I still didn't feel like the winner. It was hard for me to celebrate because I hadn't been that confident in the work that I had done. I thought Elektra, Karen and Art had all done better jobs than me.

I knew Scarlet and Maxi were for sure bottoming that week, but I didn't think I'd be any more than safe. Of course, now that I have watched it back, it's pretty clear that I absolutely kicked everyone's ass in the challenge!

I won a $2500 voucher to spend at Sydney's gorgeous House of Priscilla. That prize went a long way and I used it well. The voucher arrived the week the episode aired.

'Woo! Drag Christmas!' It was time for me to buy some organza coats, little earrings and bodysuits … I had so much fun shopping!

With a win under my belt, the finale was finally in sight. To make it all the way, though, I would need to show off my talents.

* * *

Why did no one tell me RuPaul hates magic? I somehow went from giving her exactly what she wanted to performing the sort of act she would despise no matter how well executed it was.

I began the penultimate episode of the series by saying I was going to 'fuck them up', but that wasn't exactly what happened.

When we got the 'Compete in a Talent Show' brief, I knew that I wanted to showcase something that was uniquely me – the love of magic I'd had ever since I'd seen Ken Ring perform at my sister's fifth birthday party. (Maybe if I get invited back for All Stars, I'll predict the weather based on the moon as a tribute to Ken!)

Just as I had opened the series by walking in dressed in the sort of campy look that first got me into drag, I wanted to continue to show my journey in drag through my performance in the show, and quick-change was something I had added into my act further into my drag career. It was something I wanted to show off. A great, queer, quick-change magician called Josh Hart lives in Christchurch, and Josh had made these costumes for me for an earlier performance.

Honestly, I thought it was a delicious talent. I thought it would be an exciting, fresh thing to bring to the *Drag Race* stage. I could see it going one of two ways: I could fuck it up and be sent home immediately, or I could nail it. I was utterly convinced that if I nailed it, no one would be able to beat me. Even when RuPaul told me point-blank 'I hate magic' during the walk-through, I still thought I could prove him wrong. After all, I was going onstage after Karen from Finance made one balloon animal and Art Simone put her fist in her mouth. Surely I could beat them … surely …

Performing quick-change is hard, but it is even harder to do on your own. Usually someone would help set up the costumes so they would quick-change correctly on stage, and I would have an assistant or back-up dancer who would lift up the hoop so I could execute the lightning-fast changes, but on *Drag Race*, I had to do it all by myself.

Given how hard it was to execute all by myself, the fact that my act went without a hitch was pretty rewarding. To me, it felt like a tight routine, but it didn't appear that way on the show. Thirty seconds live at a club feels like quite a short amount of time, but when it played out on television, it felt like an eternity.

I knew that if I screwed up even one of the changes, the whole act would be screwed, and they would have the perfect reason to put me in the bottom. I was pretty sure that out of Elektra and me, only one of us would make the final, because the remaining Aussie queens were such juggernauts and were so experienced outside the show. Plus, a Kiwi-on-Kiwi lip-sync was always going to provide a great moment.

Scarlet's pole routine was undoubtedly the winner, and, having nailed the routine in my opinion, I felt like I should have been in the top, just behind her. The whole episode gave me a headache. But actually, that might just have been what I was wearing on my head.

The runway category that week, 'How's Your Head Piece?', was all about headdresses and everyone had gone all out for it. I wanted to take the themes and flip them, and I didn't want to be in the same thing as anyone else. I knew that for a headdress look, most queens would go for something showgirl-y – and pretty much everyone but me did. My light-up pigtails helped me stand out from the crowd. It is still one of my favourite things I wore on the runway. I looked absolutely amazing.

It was almost as if we all wanted to get the most uncomfortable thing we could find to put on our noggins. We were backstage, waiting to walk the runway, for what felt like hours. All of the girls were moaning, complaining and asking for painkillers. It was a rough day on the runway – and it was about to get even rougher.

After our critiques, RuPaul asked each of the queens that dreaded question – who they thought should go home and why. Even though we all knew the question was coming at some point, this was one of the toughest things I had to do. I look back on it now and it seems terrible, but I had to choose someone, and I chose my sister Elektra.

I had become so close to Elektra during the shoot. I started to feel very nurturing and protective towards her. I knew she was having a hard time with some of the other girls and I wanted to be there for her. I think she is a great drag queen and a performer to be reckoned with.

Despite my personal relationship with Elektra, I had to answer the question honestly. In that moment, I wasn't just looking at the performances that episode, or even the performances across the entire season – I was weighing up the queens' entire drag careers. Art and Karen both had years of experience under their belts, and to me that counted for a lot. Elektra just hadn't been in the game as long; she hadn't lived and breathed the art of drag in quite the same way.

I knew some of her drag was lacking, only because of a lack of resources. I told her right from the outset that if I left before her she could take anything she wanted from my looks. 'If there's a theme coming up and you know that my outfit is better than what you brought, just wear it, girl!'

Still, it was an awful experience and I felt really guilty about saying Elektra's name. In Untucked, where the queens go back to the werk room to discuss what just happened on the runway while the judges deliberate, I asked Elektra if I had let her down. She simply said she was surprised I had said her.

Once we'd talked through all that drama and received a lovely surprise Zoom call from The Veronicas, we all – even Scarlet, who had so clearly won – asked production if we could make edits to our costumes, so they would be easier to lip-sync in, and we all started practising the song – well, all of us except me. I was so sure I wasn't going to end up in the bottom that I kept my boots on, I kept my incredibly blinding contact lenses in and I kept my metallic bodice on, even though I literally could not bend over in it. And yes, I kept my headpiece on, even though it was the worst thing possible to have to wear for a lip-sync. In short, I stayed in my complete look.

A producer came over to check on me. 'Are you sure you don't want to take something off and practise a little?'

'Girl. I am confident.'

Of course, that was the only week I had to lip-sync for my life.

I still think it was shady that they put me in the bottom. It is so clear that that was not how the cards fell in terms of performances on the night. Let's be real, everyone could see that my quick-change act was a hell of a lot better than the lamington-eating and the one-balloon-animal flops.

I'll happily admit that during some of the earlier challenges they could have put me up for elimination and I would have said it was fair. This time, though, no way. Not one bit. It should have been Karen and Art rather than me and Elektra, for sure.

If I had thought for a moment I'd be lip-syncing, I would have taken off those goddamn shoes right away. I could deal with the headdress and I could deal with the contacts even though I couldn't really see, but those boots meant I was glued to the spot for the whole of a pretty upbeat song.

If I'd tilted my feet in those pumps, even just a little bit, I would have rolled my ankle and that would have been it. I would have been Victoria Scone-d out of the competition. They're such dangerous shoes that, of course, I wouldn't have left them on if I had realised that my quick-change routine hadn't gone over quite as well as I had thought.

Even though I was pretty much rooted to one position the whole time, I put all my energy into my performance and gave it everything I had. I guess it must have been enough, because my sister Elektra sashayed away.

Lip-syncing against Elektra was one of the most difficult moments on the show for me. At one point, towards the end of the song, I looked at Elektra and nearly broke into tears. My question to her in Untucked – 'Have I let you down?' – kept echoing in my mind, and I couldn't help but feel like I had.

As incredible as that outfit looked, it was almost impossible to walk in, and I will definitely never wear it again. In fact, if you want to buy it – hit me up! It's of no use to me anymore. Actually, it wasn't of much use to me in that moment either.

CHAPTER 13

Getting on top

She started out a funny young queen on her local scene

She got the Ru call from the silver screen

It changed her life, that advice

Trust the gleam in your eye

Kita Mean, spread your wings and fly!

My lyrics for 'I'm a Winner, Baby' (Down Under version)

ONE OF THE GREAT things about getting to the finale of *RuPaul's Drag Race Down Under* was not just earning the chance to fight for the crown, but the amazing experience of actually getting to properly meet Michelle and RuPaul. A key part of the finale episode is that each of the remaining queens gets to sit down with the show's two legendary judges to talk about what really makes them tick. It's a chance for the judges (and the viewers) to get an insight into us as people and not just as queens.

After weeks of barely speaking to them, except when we were on the runway being judged, I was about to have a real conversation about who I am, the battles I've fought and the path that I am on.

The Jaffa lunch I had with Michelle and Ru was the first time I really got to spend proper time with either of them. (Jaffas are a Kiwi icon. They're orange-coated chocolate balls that are *so* much better than Tic Tacs.) Outside of this short lunch, I never saw Ru off set. Rhys and Michelle would sometimes come past, but Ru would arrive just before each shoot and leave immediately afterwards. She appeared out of nowhere and left the same way, like some sort of genie. I don't even know how she did it so slickly, but we never got to see behind the curtain with her and, to me, that gave her even more status and made her seem even more amazing.

In the lead-up up to our lunch, I was worried that I would feel too intimidated and find it too hard to open up to Ru and Michelle, but once I was there in front of them those nerves faded away. Sitting in front of two people I respect and admire so much, I just thought, 'This is an incredible privilege, so relax and enjoy it.'

The aim of the Jaffa lunch was to get to the core of us, to get us to reveal the most interesting and deep parts of who we are, so they could make good TV, but they did it in a way that didn't feel forced or unnatural.

I never felt like they were doing anything more than just having a classic deep-and-meaningful, like you might have with your best friend in the corner of a kitchen at a house party. It felt empathetic, their love felt genuine and their advice felt honest and impactful. Even though I couldn't escape the fact that I was doing all this in front of cameras, it still felt authentic.

There's a lot of our deep-and-meaningful that was left on the cutting-room floor, but our conversation started with my admission that the reason I try so hard to be polite and giving to people, and that I lean back on playing a comedian as a crutch, is not selflessness; it's a desperation to be loved.

'The thought of me not receiving love freaks me out,' I said. 'It's something I've always craved.'

Ru and Michelle asked if this could stem from my childhood, and I thought on that for a second. I realised that maybe this came from me not feeling seen as a child and then not *wanting* to be seen as an overweight man. For so much of my life I'd had to hide myself. It was like there had always been this struggle inside me, a desperation to be loved overshadowed and fuelled by a need to hide who I really was. And really? None of it mattered.

'You don't need to look for other people's validation,' they said. 'You have talent, and you have to recognise that and give love to yourself.'

When I heard RuPaul say, 'There is a man in your future who is going to love you like nobody's business ...' I was a little bit worried. I thought I was about to be told that being in a relationship would be the key to me sorting myself out. I was really relieved when I heard the end of that sentence: '... and that man is you!'

I began to see that, even on the show, I hadn't been treating myself kindly. The whole show, I'd felt like I wasn't performing to the best of my ability. (I still struggle with this thought even today.) But the Jaffa lunch was a moment where I could just be present and let the pressures of the past and future dissolve. I started comforting myself, 'You know what, you're all good. You're here for a reason and you're allowed to just be, without having to pick everything apart and judge yourself all the time.' I allowed myself calm, knowing that things could and would change, but what was important was that I loved myself in the moment.

* * *

The final week of *Drag Race* was a doozy. The week's main challenge involved us each adding our own verse to the iconic RuPaul song, 'I'm a Winner, Baby', then we had to learn and perform some intense choreography before showing our absolute best drag on the runway.

It's a bit hard for me to explain why I felt like I should sing instead of rap in the final challenge, but something inside me said it was time to push myself out of my comfort zone.

Coming into it, I had no idea we would end up having to write two separate verses across the competition. Having already written our own lyrics for 'Queens Down Under', I just didn't think there would be the budget for another big-production number, even though on other series of *Drag Race*, they have regularly featured writing verses for a RuPaul song in the finale. I think I'd just convinced myself that Ru wouldn't want to waste one of her hit songs on us, but happily we were blessed with the absolute smash 'I'm a Winner, Baby', and I decided to make the most of it.

I don't really consider myself a singer, not a proper one anyway, but I do know how to carry a tune. I felt pretty confident that none of the other girls could, and I wanted to differentiate myself not only from them but also from the previous rap verse I'd done on 'Queens Down Under'.

When it came to recording my verse, I laid down both a rap version and a sung version, then I asked the sound engineer to let me know which one he thought was better.

'Definitely the sung version, one hundred per cent.'

'Boom! Let's go.'

I was excited but nervous. I wasn't sure whether my singing was good or my rapping was so bad that my singing sounded better in comparison. It must have turned out all right, because a surprisingly large number of fans of the show have told me that they didn't realise it was me singing. They said they thought it sounded like RuPaul had continuing singing. But that's your girl Kita! Maybe I could be Ru's back-up if she ever loses her voice …

Anyway, I would like to thank everyone who has helped me become the singer that I am today, especially Auto-Tune, you really did the heavy lifting on that one!

My 'Best Drag' look for the finale runway all started with the wig. I had an amazing fluorescent aqua wig and I wanted to build my runway from that. I decided to make aqua the only colour in the look, so I started assembling a fully white outfit. A pair of wings were the final touch. I have been known to wear wings before, and I have these pretty incredible, gigantic golden wings, which I'd worn for the Broken Heel Festival – a *Priscilla, Queen of the Desert*–inspired event at Broken Hill in outback New South Wales, Australia. Doing a throwback to one of my recent looks seemed like the best way to conclude my runway journey.

The wings might have been the last addition to my look, but they symbolised something important for me. When I wore them, it felt like a moment of declaring that I was ready to take off. After such a mammoth journey, from my goth beginnings to becoming this angelic camp queen; from being the biggest momma on the scene to having new-found confidence as a result of my weight-loss journey; from my humble and crafty fledgling drag to being a hard-hustling business queen, I had finally realised that I am a superstar ready to spread her wings and fly.

The wings paired perfectly with the lyrics of my verse in 'I'm a Winner, Baby', so the judges got to hear about me spreading my wings and then see me do it right in front of them. I felt more beautiful than ever, and like my momentum in the show had arrived at just the right time.

After everybody got their glowing critiques, it was time for one of the most raw and vulnerable parts of the show: when RuPaul shows us a picture from our childhood and asks us to speak to our younger selves.

I've watched so many seasons of *Drag Race*, and I've seen so many people collapse into tears when they've been asked to speak to a photo of themselves as a child. Every time I thought, 'I wouldn't cry! I've seen plenty of photos of my young self. I'd keep it together.' But … nah. I cried like everyone else.

Ru held up a photo of me at four years old, one of the classic, weird glamour shots my mother had had taken of us all as children. I crumbled into tears immediately.

'What would you say to little Nick?'

'You're going to go through life and you're going to have a really weird relationship with yourself. You're going to go through some things, and you're going to get pretty unhealthy, mentally and physically. You're going to paint some pretty dark pictures for yourself. It's going to feel like it never really is going to ever really change. I'll tell you one thing now, little man – you don't give up, you do get through it. I love you so much. Let's fucking do this!'

From that tiny gay boy in Cockle Bay, moving from house to house, learning to be so uncomfortable with who he was, I had evolved into this beautiful creature on the stage, ready to fly away. Even though I had felt like so much less than the famous Aussie queens surrounding me, in that moment, I knew I had done everything I could and I was finally ready to believe: maybe I deserved this.

When they asked why I should be *Down Under*'s first drag superstar I spoke clearly and directly: 'Everything about drag has moulded me to become the businesswoman that I am, the artist that I am, but most importantly the person that I am. I will do you proud and I will represent the world and art of drag to absolute perfection. I will not take anything less.'

I said it but then I had to prove it. If I was ready to bring drag perfection, I knew I had to bring it to the final lip-sync of the season.

* * *

After the judges gave their final critiques, I was certain that only two of us would get the chance to lip-sync for the crown – maybe three, if we were really lucky.

It's hard to know exactly what the thought process behind it was – maybe they were not sure which of the four of us were the contenders while we were shooting – but for some reason, they gave us all a chance to compete in the final lip-sync. I'm so lucky they did, because I truly don't know if I would have been in the top two otherwise, and I am pretty sure the prop gag I used during our lip-sync to 'Physical' by Olivia Newton-John was what got me the crown.

It was a stunt that I had begun to plan while I was backstage during the second-to-last episode. We'd each been given an iPod (yeah, they still exist) filled with all of the possible lip-sync tracks. I'd worked out that there were only two songs left that hadn't been used, so by process of elimination, I knew that this 1980s classic would be the last number of the season. The song is especially popular in Australia, so I knew that my Aussie competitors would all know it back to front and have a routine ready to go.

Sitting in the backstage room, I felt nervous that, as the one Kiwi left, I could be defeated simply because I was the one who was least familiar with the song.

In front of me were these shelves filled with all the things we were allowed to take whenever we pleased – and Klepto Kita definitely had been taking them. There was hairspray, which I would steal every chance I got. There were nail polishes, eyelash glue and a bunch of other essential drag items, which I would pop in my pocket as I left set at the end of every shoot day.

Also on the shelves was a big first-aid kit. It was the only thing I hadn't already raided and ransacked for anything it might have to offer. Maybe some part of my brain knew stealing essential first-aid items probably wasn't the morally right thing to do … but I still wanted to have a look to see if there was anything in there I could take and convert into something for drag.

We were not allowed to talk at this point, and I just ended up staring at these rubber gloves inside the kit. I started thinking about the song, and immediately made the connection. I could put these on and perform an actual physical during the lip-sync. It was campy, it was queer, it was a gag. It could make me a winner, baby.

I took some of the rubber gloves home and practised the song.

With most songs I want to perform, I find that every time I listen to them I find something new. I was probably on the twentieth listen of 'Physical' when I heard the line about getting animal. I looked down at one of the gloves and saw that it could have a secondary purpose.

Suddenly, I was dancing around my hotel with this rubber glove udder, being a cowboy riding a sexy cow, and I just lost it. I truly found it to be the funniest thing ever. I thought to myself, 'Kita, you've done it!', then I had the most beautiful sleep of my life.

The next morning, I realised I had already blown up the only two rubber gloves I had, and once they'd been blown up, it became difficult to put them on my hands. They didn't work anymore. It was all over.

I almost gave up on the gag. It seemed too tricky to try to make it work, and I didn't want to get in trouble for stealing. Then, while we were rehearsing our group number, I started thinking, 'Fuck it. This might be the one chance I have to grab that crown.'

I got permission to go to the dairy – which is what us Kiwis call the corner shop – and I got the gloves. When the other girls saw them in my bag, it drove them crazy. 'Why does Kita have, like, a box of rubber gloves in her handbag?' they asked.

There was no way I was going to give away my gag. Apparently, there was a bit of gossip that I had some weird, kinky reason for needing them, but the only kink it was there to satisfy was my kink for winning that crown.

I'm glad they thought I was weird, because that made it even more surprising for them when they got to watch me swoop in and nail the lip-sync.

One at a time, we got up to lip-sync to 'Physical' and, as a testament to what a great song it is, no one was sick of it by the end of the fourth performance.

When the episode is screened on TV, our performances have all been spliced together, but on the day, we lip-synced one at a time in alphabetical order, while the non-lip-syncing queens watched from the back of the stage. Art went first, then Karen. Their performances were pretty similar as they both went for a 'muscle man' version of the song, and neither of them really had any major gags.

When I got up after Karen, I felt confident. I knew I had worked out something unique. And it all went great. I got laughs all the way through. I tried to play it cool, but I knew I had killed it.

When I was finished, Scarlet got up. Her take was a little sexier, but I didn't think it had many stand-out moments.

If there was an official winner for that last episode, I felt confident that it would have been me – but there was no official winner on the day. Instead, we shot four different endings, each with a different member of the final four winning. They then filmed each of us putting on the crown and walking around with the sceptre.

Once shooting wrapped, Ru gave a really nice speech. She thanked us all for our work on the show and said what a privilege it had been for her to come to our corner of the world to make her show. Then she walked off set, and that was the last time I saw her.

Michelle filmed these 'How's Your Head, Queen?' interviews with us, in which we recapped our journeys, although the ones by the top four and Elektra have never seen the light of day. That day in Auckland the Big Gay Out was on. There had been this huge internet campaign for Michelle Visage to make an appearance at the event. She is such a generous person that she did just that, travelling from set almost immediately after we finished the interviews so she was sure she made it to the festival in time.

Then we filmed our final confessionals, where we each talked about what it was like to win the crown. And then we were done.

As confident as I felt that day, I then had to leave and wait for several months before the real winner was announced. During that time, my confidence did not hang around.

* * *

The shooting period was its own kind of lockdown. It had been a gruelling schedule with barely any time off so we were ready to let loose.

On the final day of shooting, the crew had set up this whole fun wrap party for us. Everyone was ready to celebrate, and even though the party was officially meant to start at the end of the day, we were segueing into party mode as we were filming our final confessionals. I've got this great Polaroid of me with Rhys Nicholson, Scarlet Adams and Art Simone, which was taken while Karen was filming her confessional. Rhys bought us bubbles; he's an angel like that.

I was so excited to party that I didn't even pack up any of my drag. My plan was to get drunk, go to the hotel and then, after a hungover sleep-in the next day, I would go and collect my stuff.

But before the party could get properly underway: 'Beeeeep! Beep! Beeeeep! Beep!' A hideous sound suddenly howled out of every mobile phone in the city. As each person looked at their phone, the joy drained from their face. It was a notification from the government that the city would be going back into lockdown the very next day. After months of complete freedom, with no trace of Covid, a new case had appeared in the community in Auckland. Since its first appearance in 2020, we had worked so hard to eliminate the virus, and now, in February 2021, the whole city was going to step up and do it again.

After being pretty much locked in our hotel, you can imagine how excited we all were to head out and go straight … into another lockdown. In a strange turn of events, our first day of freedom also ended up being the last day of freedom (for a while, anyway) for the show's Kiwi queens.

My plan to get drunk and stay at the hotel just didn't seem possible. Instead, I got some disgusting black rubbish bags and I just threw my stuff in them there and then. With that done, a member of the production team drove me straight home. And that was the end of my *Drag Race* shooting experience. No hotel, no flash party. Instead, there was me, at my flat, like a walking zombie barely able to talk to my flatmate Trinity, and all of my beautiful drag lying there in some plastic rubbish bags.

When I eventually switched my phone back on, it vibrated for about half an hour with all of the notifications I had missed during the three weeks we'd been shooting. When it eventually calmed down, I called my mum. She was the only person I flat-out told what had happened. I remember so vividly the moment that she picked up.

I said, 'Mum, I made it all the way to the end!' Then I tried my best to explain that we'd filmed every finalist winning but she didn't quite get it.

I just wanted her to know because she had been such a supporter of me throughout my drag career, and because the money she had loaned me was the reason I was in the position I was in. I could barely get the words out. We were both in tears, and it was such a release. I felt like a little kid again, excited to tell Mum about something I had achieved.

'I'm so proud of you, darling. You deserve this,' she said.

It was overwhelming. Relieved, I collapsed on my bed. I couldn't believe it was over.

Not for the last time, I thought to myself: 'And now … we wait.'

* * *

The lockdown lasted less than a week and soon I was back doing gigs. That's when everything got a bit crazy. Everyone in the drag scene knew exactly where Anita and I had been, because it was very unusual for us to miss all the Pride gigs we did, and it kind of stuck out that our names had been removed from line-ups and posters without any announcements.

Apart from my mum, very few people knew how far I'd gone on the show. My darling flatmate and drag sister Trinity Ice knew because she lived in the house with me, so she couldn't not notice that I hadn't come home until shooting was done. Anita's husband, who works at Caluzzi as Ivanna Drink, got the call during a drag brunch that Anita was coming home, so she and a few of the girls working that day had an inkling about how far I had gone. Other than that, I kept the secret close to my fake-bosomed chest.

Once the cast was officially announced, people were desperate to know how I'd done, how Anita had done and what had gone on during the show. They were so thirsty for the tea that they would not leave me alone.

I am not someone who is good at keeping secrets – in fact, I usually crumble under the slightest amount of pressure. I knew I wouldn't be able to say, 'I signed a non-disclosure agreement, so I can't say anything.' I didn't want to leave people with nothing, so, instead, I came up with a strategy for myself.

Any time (and there were many, many times) someone backstage at a gig pressured me for information about what had gone on during filming, I would say the same thing: 'Look, it's hard for me to talk about. I'm still feeling pretty sensitive about it and really hurt. I went home first, girl. RuPaul sent me home on the first day!'

Soon the rumour that Kita had been sent home first was all through the Auckland drag scene and beyond. It even made it onto Reddit, a website where a group of rabid *Drag Race* fans share all of the juiciest spoilers they can find. People on there were *certain*. 'Kita came in really strong and confident but she just flopped right away! So sad, hope she is doing ok.'

Every elimination order prediction had me going home first, with a whole bunch of commenters backing that up.

I have to say to every one of my friends on the Auckland drag scene who took my little 'secret' and put it straight on Reddit: 'I got you, girls! Fooled your asses. Next time don't ask so many questions.'

When I told people, with full conviction, that I was the first queen to leave, they couldn't really ask more questions because they were worried they would hurt my feelings, and if I had been the first queen to go, I clearly wouldn't have much gossip anyway.

Given my legacy in the New Zealand drag scene, the idea of me getting the boot first was pretty juicy, so, of course, people wanted to talk about it. It really was delightfully camp how far the lie spread. All the while, I knew I had made it to the end, even if my belief in my actual chances at the crown was beginning to waver.

Even though I had left the last shoot feeling extremely confident, as time went on, I became more and more worried that I had not done enough. The buzz on the scene was so strong for some of the better-known Australian queens that I started to feel like the makers of the show wouldn't want me to take the crown.

The more I thought about how each episode had gone, the more it seemed as though Scarlet was going to be the winner of the show. She had had the most challenge wins, and her run across the whole show had been incredibly consistent. As soon as she'd been announced as part of the cast, though, the controversy around her previous racist performances had dominated so much of the discussion it became inescapable. As each episode screened, my idea that she would win evaporated further.

Even as that discourse continued, I still didn't feel like it was going to be me who took the title. In my view, I hadn't done enough. I didn't have the type of winner's journey that made sense in the fantasy of the show. I thought that maybe people would warm to me and be emotionally drawn to me, that they might like that I was quite sensitive and kind ... but a winner? I just couldn't see it.

Art Simone was such a superstar, and her looks were flawless all season. Karen from Finance's name was recognised all around the world, and she had so much polish that she would make a worthy winner. Meanwhile, I was the little Kiwi that could, but even on the week I won my one and only challenge, I hadn't felt confident at all. As the finale approached, though, things began to change.

* * *

Every time *Drag Race* heads towards a finale, they share a hashtag for each of the top queens, which viewers use to show their support for their chosen queen when they create, share and like social media posts.

I have no idea whether these influence the decision about who wins, but I do feel like I need to thank the fans because they definitely showed their support. The numbers were wild. The number of likes and shares for me was more than for all of the other queens combined. It worked out at about 80 per cent for #TeamKitaMean with just the remaining 20 per cent or so for the other three girls.

The whole time, I'd thought that I was an also-ran, that I was fading into the background and barely making an impact on the show. Then suddenly, it became very clear that I'd had a huge impact, that people vibed with my drag and they wanted to see me victorious.

There were pessimists out there who were saying I was only leading by default, that because of racist pasts and an unfair return to the competition, I was the only option, but … come on! Even if those things had helped, people still needed to like me. And they did. Every day I would read some of the comments of support, but it was too overwhelming to read them all.

The week the finale was due to be screened started out amazing, and then some bad news had me thinking it was about to become the shittiest week of my life.

It's worth noting that Aotearoa has had an incredible response to the Covid pandemic. We went hard and we went early. That was Aunty Cindy's (you might know her as Prime Minister Jacinda Ardern) plan and it went well. Following a tough lockdown early in 2020, we eliminated Covid in New Zealand, and for months, life was pretty much normal, just without travel. We could gig, we could party, we could kiss strangers … it was a dream! Eventually, Australia was in a similar position too.

When we filmed *Drag Race*, the Australian queens had had to quarantine for fourteen days when they arrived in the country. While the show was airing, though, our governments announced a travel bubble that would allow Aussies and Kiwis to travel freely between our two countries.

About three weeks into this new world, I was booked to travel to Australia to enjoy the finale with my sisters. I was *so* excited to be heading overseas for the first time in over a year. I was going to be joined by my drag mother Tess Tickle

and my wonderful drag sister Miss Geena, and my dear friend
Steven Oates was already over in Sydney waiting for us all to
arrive.

In the days before I went, I was advised by some TV
network people to think again. 'If you go on this trip, it might
be a long time before you can get back.'

It turned out to be good advice as things in Sydney
were about to get wild. Pandemics don't necessarily play by
the rules, and the trans-Tasman travel bubble that everyone
'down under' had been so excited about – especially drag
queens itching to perform – was about to be well and truly
burst. Delta had started to spread in New South Wales,
forcing the city of Sydney into months of harsh lockdowns. It
was devastating. I wanted so badly to watch that final episode
with my fellow top-four queens.

I cancelled the trip less than 24 hours before I was due to
get on the plane. I had been riding a high all week as so many
people on social media had come out to support me, but those
good vibes were gone. I plummeted instantly into depression.
One of the biggest moments in my life was about to happen
and my options were to either watch it at home or squashed
into my beloved but tiny Eagle bar, which is just up the road
from Caluzzi.

I didn't want this once-in-a-lifetime day to feel like any
other weekend. I had built up the idea of partying for the
finale in Sydney so much, and having it taken away by that

pesky virus left me feeling shattered. I was totally bummed out. I sat down and couldn't move. I was ready to give up on my dreams.

But then I just thought, 'Fuck it!'

I decided to throw a huge party at my house. I threw the money I would have spent living it up in Sydney on making a celebration for me and my closest pals, and it was one of the best decisions I've ever made. I bought a bunch of champagne, enough to make sure everyone there could get jolly with me. I had some great help too. Domino's gave me a massive amount of free pizza, which was very cool. Amanda Pain was there, forcing everyone to hand over their phones to avoid social media spoilers.

Watching myself be announced as the winner was completely surreal. I wish I could remember it more vividly but, I'll be honest, I was pretty drunk. Luckily Amanda had a camera filming me as I saw it happen so I can watch myself ugly-cry whenever I want to remember it.

The news took so long to sink in properly. Even when I heard RuPaul say my name, I still thought that maybe there would be some sort of tie, that I would do my winner's walk and then she would announce that everyone had won. Even after watching it happen, I was convinced that I would have the victory taken away somehow.

When it did sink in, I just plonked my head in my hands and cried for what felt like an eternity. My guests were probably worried about me … but I was happy – happier than I have ever been in my life.

After the partying at my house reached its natural peak, my friend Jordan Eskra (who is also the best DJ in the country) arranged a party bus to take us to a bar in Ponsonby called Longroom. I announced on Instagram that I was heading there, so when I arrived everyone in the bar applauded. It was amazing. I felt like an absolute superstar.

At Longroom, we were given a private section and they poured us plenty of free vodka. Unfortunately, I get drunk a lot faster these days, and I can't remember too much of the evening. All I know is, despite the disappointment of having to cancel my trip, I had one of the best weekends of my life.

The next morning, I looked at my hungover face in the mirror.

'I'm a winner, baby!'

CHAPTER 14

Delivering Kita Mean to the world

IT'S BEEN A RIDE. No matter how many cat paws they used, I don't think anyone could have predicted that the little glowing baby from Cockle Bay would go on the journey I've been on. As I look back on it, I feel nothing but gratitude for all of it – even the struggles and the people who have tried to push me down or dull my flame.

All of that played a part in getting me to where I am today. Maybe it's a little corny, but I genuinely believe that everything happens for a reason, and every little thing that has happened in my life, from being mistaken for a girl on a school trip, to getting pulled out of my car and beaten up on Dominion Road; from dropping out of chef school, to being in a band with the most offensive lyrical content you have ever heard; from turning up for my first drag show only to find that it had been cancelled, to doing a tone-deaf a cappella version of a song from *The Little Mermaid* to a crowd who hated me; from deciding to buy a business that I couldn't afford, to teaming up with my bestie to host a low-budget show with big dreams – all of it was leading me to where I am today. And where that is, is the happiest and most fulfilled I have been in my life. I'm blessed to be living comfortably. As long as my mortgage is paid and I can buy some nice drag, I'm good, and thanks to *Drag Race*, there has been enough coin coming in for me to cover those costs.

I still have not fully processed the achievement of winning the show. The crown, the sceptre, the $30,000 – it was mine. I always knew I would invest the money back into my career, so I bought some things that will come in handy for drag, especially in the time of Covid – a new computer, lights and good editing software. These were good choices, because the Zoom gigs haven't stopped and I know I can always look spectacular.

I've bought so much new drag, so many amazing wigs and shoes and costumes, that it takes two rooms to store it all. There's now a room in my house with wardrobe racks, shelves for wigs and a huge counter of jewellery. My garage is pretty much packed to the brim with all of my bigger items including my make-up station and my wings … it's a lot. I'm a glutton for new drag, and working with designers is such a joy.

I'm so lucky to be in the position that I am in. Back in the day, I used to have to rent two rooms in each place I lived; now I own my own place and have room for so much drag. I still love doing it so much, which is lucky for me because in my house, drag is everywhere I look.

I'm so grateful for every single drag artist I have met. Each has influenced me in different ways and helped to make me the queen I am today. While not all of my experiences have been positive, the negative ones just drove me to be better – and I just kept getting better.

The way things have happened, it sometimes feels almost too good to be true. Having *Drag Race* come along when it did was like the perfect storm. The way everything fell into place made me feel like I was on *The Truman Show* – but maybe that was just all the magic mushrooms I used to do.

Sometimes, I think about the alternate reality of the old pre-surgery Kita being on *Drag Race*. The truth is that the old Kita *is* the new Kita. I am the same person, and while my weight loss has given me more confidence in my personal life as Nick, I have always been this fabulous and this funny. I have always felt powerful in drag – it was the one place I didn't feel awkward or insecure. Maybe that's why I got hooked! But I've grown to love my full self, in and out of drag, so much more. I now have the ability to feel the freedom and confidence that I used to feel only in drag. I no longer see myself as lesser because of my size, and I know that professionally and romantically I deserve to be treated with respect. I'm not hiding behind a mask anymore.

I'm pleased to report that I'm in a good place in terms of my personal relationships.

Dad's still doing crosswords, though he's mostly retired. He's come down to Caluzzi, where he greatly enjoyed the rubber boobs.

Mum's still working, and I try to see her often. We recently celebrated my sister's birthday at a restaurant in town and marvelled at how far we'd all come.

I'm still friends with Lisa, Karl, Tabitha and Quentin, but our days of wild partying are over (maybe I can't speak for Karl). We're old ladies now: Sean and Lisa have a house, and Tabitha has a baby and long-term partner. We just celebrated Tabitha's birthday at a gay club in town and had an absolute riot.

I'm still in touch with Noah. He messages me and sometimes says he loves me. And the thing is, I still feel a lot of love for him too. He never asks for money these days. I think he's really taken the time to grow up. He messaged me last year to tell me that the day I took him in, even after he'd ripped me off, I saved his life: 'I know things haven't worked out for us, but I'm so thankful god put you on this earth. You are the definition of a pure soul … Even though we're not together, just know you own a piece of my heart for ever and ever.'

I was happy to hear those words. He is doing better and, as far as I can tell, he's not gambling so much these days. But if he ever tells me his dog is sick again … it's no dice! I'm confident in myself, I love the way I look, I love who I am and I won fucking *Drag Race*! I'm not going to let myself be taken advantage of again. Even better than that, I have found someone who will never take advantage of me.

I have met someone who never makes me feel unattractive or unimportant, and who would never use me for my money. He's one of the best people I have ever met in my life, and he makes me so happy. We are coming up to two years together now and I couldn't be happier.

I have had to unlearn some things, and to put my past hang-ups to one side. There was one time where he had to ask to borrow money, and even though it wasn't a huge amount, I freaked out and broke up with him on the spot. This was just a few nights before filming *Drag Race*, and even though filming the show is all-consuming, there are still many nights spent alone in your hotel room thinking about things. I realised that I had freaked out because of what someone else had done. I wasn't being fair to him as a person. It took me a while to process that not everyone is coming from the same place when it comes to borrowing money. Once I was back in the real world, I got in touch with him again. I explained why I had reacted the way I did and why money problems were a scary issue for me. Ru had said that I needed to learn to love myself, and I was coming to realise that she was right. Once I had learnt to love myself, my worth was no longer based on other people, which actually allowed me to open up and listen and understand more of where he was coming from. There had been nothing nefarious about him asking to borrow money, he just needed a small amount at that one point in time for legitimate reasons. Relax, Kita, it happens.

Aside from all of that – and a little bit because of it – it's been a strange few years. I'm sure there are many other people out there who can relate to the weirdness of achieving the most monumental thing or having some of your most significant life events occur during a global pandemic.

I have been busy and full of joy but being stuck in my house in South Auckland doing shows on Zoom did make it feel like maybe I was just living a myth. Things have begun to change, though. New Zealand's borders have reopened and I am raring to go and meet all the people around the world who connected with me during my time on the show.

I have been able to do a lot: I've released my first single, I've put together my first one-woman show, I've fronted advertising campaigns and I even did my bit promoting a vaccination drive-thru.

Now that we can travel again I have performed at Sydney Mardi Gras and I've gone on the most amazing two-month tour of the entire United States. Travelling to all of these places has made that *Down Under* crown feel so much more real.

But as much as life has changed in ways I could never have expected, a lot of things have stayed the same, and I like it that way. When I'm not touring, an average day is just as it ever was, only elevated.

I'm proud to say I do everything myself. I don't have a manager or an agent, so a lot of my mornings are spent answering emails, negotiating contracts, booking schedules and *of course* planning lewks.

Caluzzi is almost running itself these days, with the help of a powerhouse team. Ever since *Drag Race* (and the lifting of Covid restrictions), Anita and I have been busy touring and generally being fabulous. We're tight to the end, me and my girl.

Elektra left Caluzzi shortly after *Drag Race* to pursue bigger and better things, and I've been so thrilled to see her out there spreading her wings and making the most of her *Drag Race* fame.

I'm also pleased to report that Kita and Anita's Drag Wars lives on. So many fabulous Kiwi queens have got their start from Drag Wars, and it continues to be a space where people can discover the art of drag and grow their craft, which is extremely gratifying to both me and Anita.

Most of all, I'm proud I made good on little Nick's dream to one day be famous (though I'm still working on the 'rich' bit). Even though my family probably rolled their eyes whenever I said I'd be famous one day, a part of me always believed I would make it happen, and now I can say I have.

I have a lot I still want to do. I'm not stopping any time soon. Watch out, bitches, I'm coming!

xx Kita

Acknowledgments

Life is made up of every action and reaction. Sometimes there are ups and sometimes there are downs, and sometimes ups seem like downs and downs seem like ups. It's a confusing world, but one thing that has been clear and constant is the positive light and energy I have been so blessed to receive from the people I love.

I would first like to acknowledge my parents. Thank you to my beautiful mother, Bridget, for her unwavering support. She is my biggest fan and I absolutely would not be where I am today without her. Thank you to my father, Robert, who instilled his ridiculous sense of humour in me. My parents are two distinctly different personalities that came together to create a family of bold and unique kids that I am so proud to be a part of.

I am so grateful for my siblings, Craig, Matthew, Rebecca, Charlotte and Sophie. You have all taught me different things in your own ways and I feel proud to be a product of those lessons.

As blessed as I have been to have such an amazing biological family, I have been doubly blessed to have people in my life that have loved and nurtured me to the extent that I consider them my chosen family in my heart. To my drag mother, Tess Tickle – you saw the star in me and gave me the platform to let it shine. To my drag aunties Buckwheat, Kola Gin and Ling Ling; my friends Karl, Lisa, Quentin and Tabitha; my drag siblings Anita Wigl'it and Trinity Ice; and my drag daughter, Felicia – you have all been an extra-special part of creating this complex human being and I am soooo fucking grateful that our spirits are intertwined forever.

This book is a raw and honest reflection of my life up until this current moment in time, and writing it has been very therapeutic for me. It has been both a chance to celebrate and reflect, and I am nervously excited to give anyone reading this a giddy glimpse into my life. My life in lashes.

Picture section credits